DR. NOWZARADAN
DIET PLAN AND COOKBOOK
2024

Living a healthy and happy life with 1200 calories affordable recipes.
60-day meal plans suitable for any age.

JASON WILLIAMS

WE WANT TO HELP YOU EVEN MORE!

SCAN HERE THE QR CODE FOR MORE GIFT

Table of Contents

INTRODUCTION

D r. Nowzaradan's diet program is among the greatest choices if you're looking to lose weight. It focuses on maintaining an active lifestyle and eating the correct foods in the right amounts. Additionally, it suggests that you stay away from stress, alcohol and carbohydrates.

Maintaining a low-calorie diet while consuming a variety of foods high in nutrients is not impossible. Foods that aren't entirely healthful cannot be included because there is only room for 1,200 calories. Thus, doing so is necessary.

Eating a diet high in low-calorie, high-fiber fruits and vegetables, low-fat whole grains and lean proteins is crucial.

To receive one serving of fruit, you would therefore need to exchange one little rule for three-quarters of a cup of blueberries, for instance. The same numerical figures may also differ slightly from list to list due to rounding off, various scales, or various calculating methods.

However, if you consume the required amount of servings from each food group, you can be sure that your diet will be high in nutrients and low in fat and calories.

Furthermore, for some foods, it could be challenging to measure or determine the proper serving size.

BENEFITS OF
DR. NOWZARADAN'S DIET

The surgeon Dr. Nowzaradan is an American-Iranian. He is a renowned doctor who has appeared on the hit television program My 600-lb Life. His patients' lives are chronicled on the show as they shed pounds and improve their physical condition. Along with his diet, Dr. Nowzaradan also provides customized workout and dietary recommendations.

Dr. Nowzaradan created this diet to assist those who are fat or overweight in losing weight.

He stresses the need for smaller meals and eating two to three times a day, strictly monitoring calorie consumption.

This eating program can decrease surgical risk in addition to lowering obesity. Patients can in fact avoid the hazards of surgery and regain their health by reducing their caloric intake to less than 1,200 calories per day.

Anyone can lose weight using this diet strategy quickly and with few negative effects.

As they learn healthy eating habits, those following this diet plan can lower their stress levels and also have less post-operative pain thanks to it.

It is crucial to mention that Dr. Nowzaradan's diet program is intended for individuals who must drop a large amount of weight or who require surgery to lower their size. The 1,200-calorie diet plan is not long-term maintainable, even though it has many benefits.

According to a study from the Department of Pathology at the University of California, those who followed the diet had lower levels of insulin and blood sugar. Inflammation and cholesterol levels were also decreased.

Another important note is that exercise regimens are permitted under Dr. Nowzaradan's diet.

The diet plan contains a variety of nutrient-dense foods, such as those strong in fiber and protein as well as unprocessed, low-fat foods. The diet also permits low-calorie meat, fruits, vegetables, nuts and low-calorie nuts in addition to healthful meals.

You should stay away from processed meats, though. Fried meats and sauces with added sugar are also prohibited. These limitations are practical and are meant to guarantee that you're eating a balanced diet.

The diet calls for the dieter to consume approximately 1200 calories a day and promotes sensible eating practices and makes the dieter more conscious of portion size.

By reducing fat, limiting carbohydrates and boosting fiber you may lose up to 30 pounds in four weeks with the help of this book.

TRICKS AND TIPS
TO STAY ON THE NOWZARADAN DIET

The diet program emphasizes a balanced diet in addition to calorie restriction. This is to consume more energy than the calories ingested burning more fat.

It is not an easy path, it requires perseverance and reliability. Fortunately, there are many diet strategies available to assist people in achieving their optimum weight.

The diet restricts snacking because it can result in binge eating. Dieters should not, however, completely stop nibbling but stay on track by eating tiny snacks in between meals.

This diet avoids high-fat, high-calorie items in favor of low-calorie, healthful foods. Additionally, reducing calories to 1200 or less has a number of unfavorable side effects, such as lowering your metabolism and changing your hormones that control hunger.

The Nowzaradan Diet Plan takes preparation and planning, just like any other diet and, it's best to speak with a dietician or physician before beginning the diet in order to succeed. Furthermore, those who are exceedingly fat should only turn to the Nowzaradan Diet Plan as a last choice. There are other additional, more potent ways to lose weight.

A few regulations and recommendations:

- Eating only tiny portions;
- Avoid high calories foods like processed snacks, sweets and starchy vegetables;
- Abstain from alcoholic and calorie-dense beverages.

It's also crucial to keep in mind that the diet necessitates a considerable lifestyle adjustment, including a dedication to altering eating habits prior to surgery and maintaining a healthy lifestyle afterward.

FOODS TO EAT

WHAT YOU SHOULD NOT EAT

Below are the highlights of what you should be eating to reach your goals.

Fruits and Vegetables: Fruits and vegetables have been proven time and time again to have many health benefits. They are also low in calories and packed with nutrients, vitamins and minerals that your body needs. It is vital that you eat five servings of fruits and vegetables every day.

Whole Grains: Eating whole grains is one of the best ways to gain more nutrients in your diet. Whole grains are packed with B vitamins, iron and numerous other minerals that are vital for a healthy body. They also provide you with a feeling of fullness so you don't overeat because it's hard to stop eating before you have finished all the food on your plate.

Lean protein: Protein is vital for building muscle, repairing damaged tissue and enhancing your metabolism. It also helps maintain an active lifestyle. If you are looking to lose weight, it is essential that you add lean protein such as fish, chicken breast and tofu to your diet.

Healthy Fats: Healthy fats can be found in coconut oil and olive oil. They are not only healthy for you but they also go great with most healthy foods. Healthy fats can help your body absorb the fat-soluble vitamins A and D that your body needs to help keep your immune system strong. Fats are vital for the proper growth and development of your body. Without them, you could easily develop a diet deficiency that can gradually lead to health problems.

One rule you will have to remember is that eating healthy should not mean eating carbs. Carbohydrates are one of the worst things you can have in your diet if you are looking to lose weight. They can actually make you gain weight over time if they are not consumed in small amounts from time to time.

There are a few other foods that you should not eat if you are looking to lose weight. Some of these bad foods include:

Salty Foods: These are not only bad for you, but they are a waste at the same time. Not only does eating too much salt cause problems with your blood pressure, but it also makes you feel bloated and can lead to stomach cramps if eaten in large amounts.

Yeast breads: Yeast breads are one of the worst things you can have in your diet. They are packed with carbs, which is something that you should avoid while dieting.

Chicken and turkey skin: These are the skin from chicken or turkey. They contain loads of bad fats that can lead to health problems in the future.

Chicken nuggets and tenders: These are made out of breast meat, but they are sometimes pumped with growth hormones to make them larger.

Unhealthy fats: Olive oil is an example of healthy fat, but there are also unhealthy fats such as trans fats found in fried food or a lot of processed foods.

WHY DO CALORIES MATTER?

When it comes to maintaining a healthy weight, the calories that you consume are just as important as the calories that you burn. There are a lot of people who try to lose weight on low-calorie diets and that can lead to permanent damage to their body or even death.

You will have to make sure that you don't starve yourself while dieting because it forces your body into a state of starvation. That can slow down your metabolism and cause your body to store more fat in order to start a new cycle of life.

Your body will only burn calories when it needs to, which is why it is not uncommon for people who starve themselves to actually gain weight. Most of the time, this weight gain is in the form of fat instead of muscle mass as it normally would be because their bodies have lost all muscle and most of their energy.

60 DAYS MEAL PLAN

Meal Plan	Breakfast	Lunch	Dinner
DAY-1	Canadian Bacon Eggs Benedict	Asian Flank Steak with Edamame and Soba	Beef and Bell Pepper Frittata
DAY-2	Cauliflower-Based Waffles	Baked Vegetables	Garlic Pumpkin Soup with Fried Sage
DAY-3	Cheese Waffles	Buffalo Wings	Bean Soup
DAY-4	Chorizo Frittata	Curried Chicken Meatballs with Rice	Garlic Squash Broccoli Soup
DAY-5	Mexican Eggs	Chicken, Tomato and Green Beans	Chicken Lentil Stew
DAY-6	Sesame and Poppy Seed Bagels	Citrus Pork	Cauliflower Soup with Onion
DAY-7		Green Bean Casserole	Chicken with Garlic and Fennel
DAY-8	Ham and Egg Casserole	Nut-Crusted Chicken Breasts	Balsamic Chili Roast
DAY-9	Ginger Snaps	Roast Pork Loin with Rosemary and Garlic	Chicken Tikka
DAY-10	Morning Herbed Eggs	Chicken and Cheese Stuffed Peppers	Spinach Chicken Stew
DAY-11	Poached Eggs	Chicken Relleno Casserole	Beef and Bell Pepper Frittata
DAY-12	Jackfruit Vegetable Fry	Coconut Fried Shrimp with Cilantro Sauce	Classic Mediterranean Fish Stew
DAY-13	Goat Cheese Frittata with Asparagus	Chicken with Potatoes Olives and Sprouts	Beans & Lentil Soup
DAY-14	Sesame and Poppy Seed Bagels	Cod Salad with Mustard	Lamb Stew
DAY-15	Cheese Waffles	Beef and Mushroom Meatloaf	Cabbage and Beef Steaks
DAY-16	Ginger and Pumpkin Pie	Chicken and Sausage Gumbo	Chicken Lentil Stew
DAY-17	Poached Eggs	Feta and Mozzarella Chicken	Chicken Tikka
DAY-18	Chorizo Frittata	Steak Fajitas	Beef and Bell Pepper

			Frittata
DAY-19	Ginger Snaps	Tuna Noodle Casserole	Balsamic Chili Roast
DAY-20	Jackfruit Vegetable Fry	Chicken Lentil Stew	Cream Broccoli Kale Soup
DAY-21	Fat-Free Fries	Asian Flank Steak with Edamame and Soba	Classic Mediterranean Fish Stew
DAY-22	Goat Cheese and Rutabaga Puffs	Hearty Pork Stew	Creamy Chicken Fried Rice
DAY-23	Ginger Snaps	Garlicky Ginger Potato and Rice Soup	Mixed Grains Chili
DAY-24	Chorizo Frittata	Baked Vegetables	Chicken Lentil Stew
DAY-25	Creamy Oatmeal	Tuna Noodle Casserole	Cauliflower Soup with Onion
DAY-26	Bean Soup	Steak Fajitas	Beef & Mushroom Soup
DAY-27	Cherry Clafouti	Healthy Vegetable Soup	Cumin Pork and Beans
DAY-28	Sesame and Poppy Seed Bagels	Beef and Mushroom Meatloaf	Cream Broccoli Kale Soup
DAY-29	Soft Banana Bread	Baked Vegetables	Beef and Bell Pepper Frittata
DAY-30	Goat Cheese and Rutabaga Puffs	Spinach Chicken Stew	Mixed Grains Chili
DAY-31	Mushroom and Cheese Cauliflower Risotto	Garlic Squash Broccoli Soup	Meatballs Curry
DAY 32	Sweet Chia Bowls	Creamy Sweet Potato Onion Curry Soup	Classic Mediterranean Fish Stew
DAY-33	Coconut Crepes with Vanilla Cream	Asian Flank Steak with Edamame and Soba	Balsamic Chili Roast
DAY 34	Jackfruit Vegetable Fry	Buffalo Wings	Beef and Bell Pepper Frittata
DAY-35	Chorizo Frittata	Cod Salad with Mustard	Chicken Tikka
DAY-36	Canadian Bacon Eggs Benedict	Chicken with Potatoes Olives and Sprouts	Cabbage and Beef Steaks
DAY 37	Cauliflower-Based Waffles	Chicken Lentil Stew	Spinach Chicken Stew
DAY-38	Crabmeat Frittata with Onion	Tuna Noodle Casserole	Cabbage and Beef Steaks
DAY-39	Ham and Egg Casserole	Garlicky Ginger Potato and Rice Soup	Bean Soup
DAY-40	Jackfruit Vegetable Fry	Healthy Vegetable Soup	Beef and Bell Pepper Frittata
DAY-41	Goat Cheese and Rutabaga Puffs	Creamy Sweet Potato Soup	Black Bean Stew with Mango and Onion

DAY-42	Ginger Snaps	Hearty Pork Stew	Tomato Chickpeas Stew
DAY-43	Spinach Nests with Eggs and Cheese	Fish and Shrimp Soup	Balsamic Chili Roast
DAY-44	Snazzy Baked Eggs	Buffalo Wings	Beef and Bell Pepper Frittata
DAY-45	Goat Cheese and Rutabaga Puffs	Cod Salad with Mustard	Beef and Bell Pepper Frittata
DAY-46	Chili Omelet with Avocado	Chicken Lentil Stew	Mixed Grains Chili
DAY-47	Jackfruit Vegetable Fry	Asian Flank Steak with Edamame and Soba	Cabbage and Beef Steaks
DAY-48	Sweet Chia Bowls	Steak Fajitas	Cauliflower Soup with Onion
DAY-49	Crabmeat Frittata with Onion	Healthy Vegetable Soup	Easy & Delicious Beef Stew
DAY-50	Chili Omelet with Avocado	Mixed Lentil Stew	Cream Broccoli Kale Soup
DAY-51	Coconut Crepes with Vanilla Cream	Tuna Noodle Casserole	Meatballs Curry
DAY-52	Avocado Tuna Bites	Garlicky Ginger Potato and Rice Soup	Beef and Bell Pepper Frittata
DAY-53	Poached Eggs	Hearty Pork Stew	Balsamic Chili Roast
DAY-54	Goat Cheese and Rutabaga Puffs	Easy Mixed Vegetable Noodle Bowl	Beef and Bell Pepper Frittata
DAY-55	Sesame and Poppy Seed Bagels	Tuna Noodle Casserole	Bean Soup
DAY-56	Chili Omelet with Avocado	Garlic French Onion Soup	Chicken and Chorizo Traybake
DAY-57	Canadian Bacon Eggs Benedict	Beef and Mushroom Meatloaf	Cabbage and Beef Steaks
DAY-58	Sweet Chia Bowls	Garlicky Ginger Potato and Rice Soup	Brown Basmati Rice Pilaf
DAY-59	Coconut Crepes with Vanilla Cream	Hearty Pork Stew	Beef and Bell Pepper Frittata
DAY-60	Chili Omelet with Avocado	Healthy Vegetable Soup	Balsamic Chili Roast

BREAKFAST RECIPES

1. Canadian Bacon Eggs Benedict

- Serving Size: 2
- Preparation Time: 10 minutes
- Cooking Time: 20 minutes

Ingredients:
- 1 teaspoon of white wine vinegar
- 2 large eggs
- 4 Canadian bacon slices
- 1 tablespoon of fresh parsley chopped

Directions:
1. In a large skillet, heat it to medium heat. Cook the bacon for about 3-4 minutes on each side. Transfer to a towel to absorb any excess fat. Boil the vinegar and water in a pot on high heat. Then reduce it to simmer.
2. Crack eggs into bowls and then gently place eggs into boiling water. Allow to simmer for a couple of minutes. Utilize a spoon with a perforated hole to take the egg out of the water onto the cloth to air dry.
3. Put the bacon on two plates. Each plate should be topped with an egg. Sprinkle with chopped parsley.
4. Serve and enjoy!

Nutrition: Calories: 250, Carbs: 1.4g, Fat: 9 g, Protein: 18g

2. Cauliflower-Based Waffles

- Serving Size: 2
- Preparation Time: 15 minutes
- Cooking Time: 25 minutes

Ingredients:

- 1 cup of zucchini chopped and squeezed
- 2 green onions
- 1 tbsp of olive oil
- 2 eggs
- 1/3 cup of Parmesan cheese
- 1 cup of mozzarella, grated
- Half-head cauliflower
- 1 teaspoon of garlic powder
- 1 tbsp of sesame seeds
- 2 teaspoons thyme, chopped

Directions:

1. Cut the cauliflower into florets. Mix the pieces in the food processor and then pulse until rice is created. Transfer to a kitchen towel and press down to remove excess moisture. Return to your food processor and add the zucchini, green onions and thyme. Pulse until smooth.
2. Transfer into an empty bowl. Add all the other prepared ingredients and mix well. Allow sitting for 10 minutes
3. Warm the waffle iron, then spread it all over the mixture. Cook until golden brown in about 5 minutes.
4. Serve and enjoy!

Nutrition:

- Calories: 260, Carbs: 7.2g , Fat: 21g , Protein: 32g

3. Cheese Waffles

- Serving Size: 8
- Preparation Time: 15 minutes
- Cooking Time: 20 minutes

Ingredients:

- 2 garlic cloves, minced
- Salt and black pepper, to taste
- 1 cup of frozen spinach
- 2 cups of ricotta cheese, crumbled
- ½ cup of low-fat parmesan cheese, grated
- 1 cup of part-skim mozzarella cheese, shredded
- 2 eggs, beaten

Directions:

1. Add eggs, garlic cloves, ricotta cheese and spinach in a large bowl. Now, add mozzarella cheese, parmesan cheese, salt and pepper.
2. Whisk properly.
3. Pour the prepared batter on the waffle iron and cook for about 5 minutes.
4. Take out and serve hot with maple syrup on the top.

Nutrition:

- Calories: 225
- Carbs: 3.9g
- Fat: 7g
- Protein: 10.2g

4. Chorizo Frittata

- Serving Size: 4
- Preparation Time: 30 minutes
- Cooking Time: 40 minutes

Ingredients:

- 1 chorizo sausage, sliced
- 1/2 cup of kale
- 1 tbsp of butter
- 1/2 cup of cheese from Cotija shred
- Half red bell pepper chopped
- 4 eggs, salt and black pepper to taste
- 1 tsp of chipotle paste
- 1 green onion chopped

Directions:

1. Oil and heat the pan and cook the onion. Add chorizo sausage, chipotle paste and bell pepper. Cook for about 5-7 minutes.
2. Mix the eggs in the bowl and then season with salt and black pepper.
3. Put the kale in and boil for about 2 minutes. Incorporate eggs.
4. Sprinkle the mixture evenly across the skillet, then place it in the oven. Cook for about 8 mins at 350 F until the top of the pan is cooked and golden.
5. Sprinkle crumbled cotija cheese on top and bake for another 3 moments until the cheese is completely melted.
6. Cut and enjoy while warm.

Nutrition:

- Calories: 353
- Carbs: 7.3g
- Fat: 31g
- Protein: 24g

5. Chili Omelet with Avocado

- Serving Size: 2
- Preparation Time: 5 minutes
- Cooking Time: 15 minutes

Ingredients:

- 2 tsp of olive oil
- 1 ripe avocado, chopped
- 2 spring onions chopped
- 2 spring garlic, chopped
- 4 eggs 1 cup of buttermilk
- 2 tomatoes, sliced
- 1 pepper with green chili, chopped
- 2 tablespoons fresh cilantro, chopped
- black pepper and salt to taste

Directions:

1. Mix the buttermilk, eggs, salt and black pepper. Oil and heat the pan and cook the garlic and onions until they are tender. Pour the dish into the pan and employ a spatula for smoothing the surface.
2. Include chili pepper, cilantro, avocado, tomatoes and chili pepper on the other side of the egg dish. Fold it in half, then eventually cut it into pieces. Serve immediately.

Nutrition:

- Calories: 384
- Carbs: 11g
- Fat: 32g
- Protein: 19g

6. Coconut Crepes with Vanilla Cream

- Serving Size: 4
- Preparation Time: 20 minutes
- Cooking Time: 35 minutes

Ingredients:

- 5 large eggs
- ¼ coconut flour
- 1 tsp of sugar-free cocoa powder
- ¼ cup of flax milk
- 2 tbsp of coconut oil, melted
- Vanilla cream
- ¼ cup of butter
- 2 tbsp of erythritol
- ½ tsp of vanilla extract
- ½ cup of coconut cream

Directions:

1. Beat the prepared eggs with a whisk in a bowl. Add the flax milk, cocoa powder, coconut flour and coconut oil and mix until well combined. Oil and heat the pan to spread the dough around the skillet and cook the crepe for 2-3 minutes.
2. Melt the butter in a large-sized saucepan. Pour in the coconut cream and erythritol, reduce the heat to low and let the sauce simmer for 8 minutes.
3. Turn the heat off and stir in the vanilla extract. Drizzle the sauce over the crepes and serve.

Nutrition:

- Calories: 108, Carbs: 3g , Fat: 23g , Protein: 10g

7.   Crabmeat Frittata with Onion

- Serving Size: 2
- Preparation Time: 10 minutes
- Cooking Time: 30 minutes

Ingredients:

- 1 tbsp of olive oil
- 1/2 onion chopped
- Black pepper and salt to taste
- 3 oz crabmeat, chopped
- 4 large eggs, lightly beaten
- 1/2 cup of sour cream

Directions:

1. Set a pan on moderate heat and heat the oil to cook the onion. Add the crabmeat and cook for 2 minutes. Add salt and pepper to taste.
2. Mix the sour cream and the eggs. Transfer the egg mixture to the skillet. Place the pan in the oven to cook for about 17 mins at 350 F or until the eggs are cooked.
3. Cut into wedges and serve.

Nutrition:

- Calories: 261
- Carbs: 6.5g
- Fat: 26g
- Protein: 23g

8. Creamy Oatmeal

- Serving Size: 4
- Preparation Time: 15 minutes
- Cooking Time: 10 minutes

Ingredients:

- 1 cup of berries of choice
- 2 cups of oats, old fashioned
- 1 and one-third cup of almonds, sliced
- 3 and one-fourth cups of water
- 1 tablespoon of ground cinnamon
- 2 medium bananas

Directions:

1. Crush the bananas thoroughly until smooth. Empty the water into a saucepan and incorporate the mashed banana. Combine the oats in the pan and heat until the water bubbles.
2. Adjust the temperature of the burner to low and continue to warm for approximately 7 minutes.
3. Remove from heat and top with the ground cinnamon, berries and sliced almonds.
4. Serve immediately and enjoy!

Nutrition:

- Calories: 295
- Carbs: 52g
- Fat: 21g
- Protein: 18g
- Sugar: 12g

9. Goat Cheese Frittata with Asparagus

- Serving Size: 2
- Preparation Time: 15 minutes
- Cooking Time: 35 minutes

Ingredients:

- 1 tbsp of olive oil
- 1/2 onion chopped
- 1 cup of asparagus chopped
- 4 eggs, beaten
- 1/2 habanero pepper, minced
- Red pepper and salt, to taste
- 3/4 cup of goat cheese, crumbled
- 1 tbsp of chopped parsley

Directions:

1. Preheat the oven to a heat of 350 F. Sauté the onion in olive oil at medium-high temperature until it is caramelized, about 6-8 minutes. In the asparagus, simmer until soft, around 5 minutes. Add habanero peppers and eggs. Season with salt and red pepper.
2. Cook until eggs are cooked. Sprinkle the goat cheese and chopped parsley on top of the frittata. Bake for 20 minutes.
3. Serve and enjoy!

Nutrition:

- Calories: 192, Carbs: 8.3g, Fat: 37g, Protein: 32g

10. Ham and Egg Casserole

- Serving Size: 4
- Preparation Time: 5 minutes
- Cooking Time: 25 minutes

Ingredients:

- 4 red potatoes, medium
- 1 cup of chopped ham
- 10 huge eggs
- 1 teaspoon of salt and pepper
- ½ diced onion
- 2 cups of shredded cheese
- 1 cup of skim milk

Directions:

1. Spray inside of the prepared instant pot with cooking spray and in another dish then add eggs and milk till blended.
2. Put the rest of the ingredients in there, mix them and then cover with foil.
3. Add an insert and then a casserole dish on top of there.
4. Cook it on manually for 25 minutes with a natural pressure release.
5. Serve immediately with toppings.

Nutrition:

- Calories: 221, Carbs: 15g, Fat: 10g, Protein: 22g

- Serving Size: 6
- Preparation Time: 5 minutes
- Cooking Time: 5 minutes

Ingredients:

- 2 seeded and chopped red bell peppers
- 1/8 teaspoon of. cayenne pepper
- 2 cups of finely chopped cherry tomatoes
- Salt
- 1 tablespoon of olive oil
- 3 cups of seeded and chopped firm jackfruit
- 2 tablespoons of chopped fresh basil leaves
- 1/8 teaspoon of ground turmeric
- 2 finely chopped small onions

Directions:

1. Oil and heat the pan to cook the onions, tomatoes and bell peppers for 5 minutes.
2. Then add the salt, cayenne pepper, jackfruit, turmeric and cook for 8 minutes.
3. Garnish the meal with basil leaves and serve warm.

Nutrition:

- Calories: 326
- Carbs: 5g
- Fat: 1.8g
- Protein: 7g

12. Mexican Eggs

- Serving Size: 8
- Preparation Time: 5 minutes
- Cooking Time: 2 hours

Ingredients:

- 12 ounces of low-fat cheese, shredded
- 1 garlic clove, minced
- 1 cup of nonfat sour cream
- 10 eggs
- Olive oil cooking spray
- 5 ounces of canned green chilies, drained
- 10 ounces tomato sauce, sodium-free
- ½ teaspoon of chili powder
- Black pepper to the taste

Directions:

1. In a bowl, mix the eggs with the cheese, sour cream, chili powder, black pepper, garlic, green chilies and tomato sauce.
2. Whisk and pour into your slow cooker after you've greased it with cooking oil, cover and cook on low for 2 hours.
3. Serve.

Nutrition:

- Calories: 557, Carbs: 18.8g, Fat: 27.5g, Protein: 20.9g

13. Morning Herbed Eggs

- Serving Size: 2
- Preparation Time: 5 minutes
- Cooking Time: 15 minutes

Ingredients:

- 1 spring onion finely chopped
- 2 tbsp of butter
- 1 teaspoon of fresh thyme
- 4 eggs
- 1/2 tsp of sesame seeds
- 2 cloves of garlic, chopped
- 1/2 cup of chopped parsley
- 1/2 cup of chopped sage
- 1/4 tsp of cayenne pepper
- Black pepper and salt to taste

Directions:

1. Add garlic, parsley thyme and sage and stir fry in 30-second intervals in a pan at medium temperature. Make sure to crack the eggs in the skillet.
2. Serve the eggs with a drizzle of cayenne pepper and sesame seeds.

Nutrition:

- Calories: 227
- Carbs: 4g
- Fat: 22g
- Protein: 13g

14. Mushroom and Cheese Cauliflower Risotto

- Serving Size: 4
- Preparation Time: 15 minutes
- Cooking Time: 25 minutes

Ingredients:

- 3 tbsp of olive oil
- 1 onion chopped
- 1/4 cup of vegetable broth
- 1/3 cup of Parmesan cheese
- 4 tbsp of heavy cream
- 3 tbsp of chopped chives.
- 2 lbs mushrooms, sliced
- 1 large head cauliflower, break into florets
- 2 tbsp of chopped parsley, cut

Directions:

1. In the food processor, blend the cauliflower florets until they achieve a rice-like texture. Heat 2 tbsp of oil in a saucepan. Add the mushrooms and cook on moderate heat for approximately 3 minutes.
2. Mix in the broth and the cauliflower, then cook until the broth has been completely absorbed, about 7-8 minutes. Mix in the heavy cream as well as Parmesan cheese.
3. Sprinkle with parsley and chives to serve.

Nutrition:

- Calories: 213, Carbs: 5.3g, Fat: 21g, Protein: 10g

- Serving Size: 2
- Preparation Time: 10 minutes
- Cooking Time: 5 minutes

Ingredients:

- 2 eggs
- 2 slices of low-fat mozzarella
- 1 cup of mayonnaise
- 1 bell pepper, halved
- 3 tablespoons sugar-free orange juice
- 1 teaspoon of lemon juice
- 1 teaspoon of turmeric powder
- 1 teaspoon of mustard
- 1 tablespoon of sugar
- 1 cup of water

Directions:

1. Crack eggs into the bell pepper cups and add mozzarella slices.
2. Add water and then add the cups off, cover and cook on low for four minutes.
3. In a bowl, mix the other ingredients and then divide the poached eggs between plates, add the sauce over them and then serve!

Nutrition:

- Calories: 72, Carbs: 21g, Fat: 5g, Protein: 5g

16. Rolled Smoked Salmon with Avocado

- Serving Size: 2
- Preparation Time: 10 minutes
- Cooking Time: 10 minutes

Ingredients:

- 2 tbsp of cream cheese, softened
- 1 lime, squeezed, zested and juiced
- 1/2 avocado, pitted, peeled
- 1 tbsp of mint and chopped
- Salt to taste
- 2 slices of smoked salmon

Directions:

1. Mash the avocado using a fork in the bowl. Add the mint, lime juice zest, cream cheese and salt and mix until well combined. Place each salmon piece onto a plastic wrap and fill with cream cheese mixture.
2. Refrigerate the wrapped mixture for 2 minutes. Then take the plastic off, cut each wrap's sides and cut pieces into the quarter-inch wheel.
3. Serve.

Nutrition:

- Calories: 321
- Carbs: 3g
- Fat: 31g
- Protein: 50g

17. Scrambled Eggs with Mushrooms and Spinach

- Serving Size: 2
- Preparation Time: 5 minutes
- Cooking Time: 10 minutes

Ingredients:

- 2 egg whites
- 1 slice whole wheat toast
- ½ cup of sliced fresh mushrooms
- Fat-free American cheese
- Pepper to taste
- 1 teaspoon of olive oil
- 1 cup of chopped fresh spinach
- 1 whole egg

Directions:

1. Oil and heat the pan, add mushrooms and spinach. Cook for 2-3 minutes.
2. Mix egg whites and cheese. Season with pepper.
3. Cook the egg mixture.
4. Serve and enjoy with a piece of whole wheat toast.

Nutrition:

- Calories: 183
- Carbs: 21.8g
- Fat: 11.8g
- Protein: 24.3g

18. Sesame and Poppy Seed Bagels

- Serving Size: 4
- Preparation Time: 20 minutes
- Cooking Time: 30 minutes

Ingredients:

- 1/4 cup of Coconut flour
- 6 eggs
- 1 cup of a meal of flaxseed
- 1/2 teaspoon of onion powder
- 1/2 1 teaspoon of garlic powder
- 1 teaspoon of dried oregano
- 1 tsp of sesame seeds
- 1 teaspoon of poppy seeds

Directions:

1. Combine the coconut flour eggs, 1 teaspoon of flaxseed meal, 1/2 cup of water, garlic powder, onion powder, oregano and onion powder.
2. Pour the mix into a donut tray that has been greased. Sprinkle with sesame and poppy seeds. Baking the bread for about 20 minutes a 350 F.
3. Cool for 5 minutes before serving.

Nutrition:

- Calories: 180, Carbs: 3.3g , Fat: 24g, Protein: 20g

19. Snazzy Baked Eggs

- Serving Size: 4
- Preparation Time: 5 minutes
- Cooking Time: 8 minutes

Ingredients:

- 4 eggs
- 4 slices of meat, fish, or veggies of choice
- 4 slices of cheese or a shot of cream
- 4 garnishes of fresh herbs of choice
- Cooking oil

Directions:

1. Add a cup of water and then prepare your ramekins by setting olive oil on the bottom of it and then the meat and veggies.
2. Break an egg and then add the cheese and creak of your choice.
3. Add it into the pressure cooker for low heat, for 8 minutes.
4. Remove and put them on a little plate.

Nutrition:

- Calories: 216
- Carbs: 8g
- Fat: 4g
- Protein: 8g

20. Soft Banana Bread

- Serving Size: 4
- Preparation Time: 10 minutes
- Cooking Time: 4 hours

Ingredients:

- 2 eggs
- ½ teaspoon of baking soda
- 3 bananas, peeled and mashed
- 2 cups of whole wheat flour
- 1 teaspoon of baking powder
- 2 tablespoons olive oil

Directions:

1. In a bowl, mix the eggs with the oil, flour, baking powder and baking soda and whisk well.
2. Add bananas, stir the batter, pour it into your greased slow cooker, cover and cook on Low for 4 hours.
3. Slice the bread, divide it between plates and serve.

Nutrition:

- Calories: 100
- Carbs: 68.7g
- Fat: 10.1g
- Protein: 10.2g

21. Spinach Nests with Eggs and Cheese

- Serving Size: 1
- Preparation Time: 15 minutes
- Cooking Time: 25 minutes

Ingredients:

- 1 tbsp of olive oil
- 1 tbsp of dried dill
- 1 lb spinach, chopped
- 1 tbsp of pine nuts
- Black pepper and salt to taste
- 1/4 cup of feta cheese, crumbled
- 2 eggs

Directions:

1. Sauté the spinach in the olive oil at medium-low temperatures for 5 minutes. Sprinkle with salt and pepper and put aside.
2. Prepare a baking sheet by coating it with cooking spray, form two (firm and distinct) spinach nests on the baking sheet and then crack an egg inside each nest.
3. Sprinkle with feta and then sprinkle with dill. Cook for about 15 mins a 350 F until the egg whites are settled and the yolks remain running.
4. Serve the nests on plates decorated with pine nuts.

Nutrition:

- Calories: 120
- Carbs: 5.4g
- Fat: 22g
- Protein: 18g

22. Sweet Chia Bowls

- Serving Size: 4
- Preparation Time: 10 minutes
- Cooking Time: 2 hours

Ingredients:

- 1 teaspoon of cinnamon powder
- 2 cups of non-fat milk
- 1 tablespoon of maple syrup
- 2 tablespoons chia seeds
- 2 bananas, peeled and sliced
- 1 teaspoon of sugar
- 1 teaspoon of vanilla extract
- 1 cup of brown rice

Directions:

1. Mix the maple syrup, and milk with the bananas and the other ingredients and cook for 2 hours.
2. Serve.

Nutrition:

- Calories: 153
- Carbs: 63.4g
- Fat: 3.5g
- Protein: 9.3g

23. Asian Flank Steak with Edamame and Soba

- Serving Size: 4
- Preparation Time: 10 minutes
- Cooking Time: 30 minutes

Ingredients:

- ¼ pound of soba noodles
- 1 teaspoon of canola oil
- 4 ounces of trimmed beef flank steak, sliced thinly across the grain
- 1 ½ tablespoons of lime juice
- 1 ½ tablespoons of low-sodium teriyaki sauce
- 1 ½ tablespoons of garlic and chili paste
- ½ teaspoon of cornstarch
- ½ teaspoon of sesame oil
- ½ red pepper, julienned
- 2 green onions, diagonally cut
- 8 snow peas, cut into strips
- ¼ cup of shredded carrot
- 1 cup of frozen edamame, thawed
- 1 tablespoon of fresh minced ginger root
- ¼ cup of cilantro

Directions:

1. Cook soba noodles according to package directions.
2. While noodles are cooking, heat sauté pan with oil. Add steak to the pan and cook until just done (approximately 2 minutes).
3. Whisk lime juice, teriyaki, chili paste, ginger root, cornstarch and sesame oil together to form a sauce. Add red pepper, onions, snow peas and carrot to the pan and add prepared sauce. Cook for 2 minutes.
4. Add beef and juices from the plate back into the pan. Add edamame and toss to heat through. Add soba noodles and toss.
5. Garnish with fresh cilantro and serve.

Nutrition:

- Calories: 401
- Carbs: 31g
- Fat: 4g
- Protein: 17g

24. Baked Vegetables

- Serving Size: 8
- Preparation Time: 5 minutes
- Cooking Time: 25 minutes

Ingredients:

- 1 onion sliced into wedges
- 6 carrots sliced
- 4 potatoes sliced
- 6 chicken breast fillets sliced into cubes
- 1 teaspoon of thyme
- Pepper to taste
- ½ cup of water

Directions:

1. Preheat your oven to 400°F. Toss onion, carrots and potatoes in a baking pan. Arrange chicken on top.
2. In a bowl, combine thyme, pepper and water, add to the chicken and bake for 1 hour.
3. Transfer to a food container and refrigerate for up to 2 days.
4. Reheat before serving.

Nutrition:

- Calories: 240
- Carbs: 25g
- Fat: 3.5g

25. Buffalo Wings

- Serving Size: 4
- Preparation Time: 20 minutes
- Cooking Time: 50 minutes

Ingredients:

- 12 jumbo chicken wings, skin removed
- 1 tablespoon of black peppercorns
- 1 medium onion
- 1 stalk of celery
- 1 head of garlic, halved
- 1 batch of Hot and Spicy Marinade
- 2 tablespoons of Creole seasoning or spicy rub

Directions:

1. Place chicken wings in a heavy deep pot and add peppercorns, onions, celery and garlic; cook for 12 minutes.
2. Remove the chicken from the water and cool.
3. Coat in Hot and Spicy Marinade and let sit overnight.
4. Preheat oven to 350°F.
5. Spray sheet pan with nonstick spray and lay wings in a single layer on the pan, season with Creole and bake for 12 minutes.
6. Serve with the prepared celery sticks and low-fat blue cheese dressing.

Nutrition:

- Calories: 180, Carbs: 12g, Fat: 5g, Protein: 21g

26. Curried Chicken Meatballs with Rice

- Serving Size: 4
- Preparation Time: 10 minutes
- Cooking Time: 20 minutes

Ingredients:

- 1 pound of lean ground chicken
- ½ cup of yellow onion, minced
- ¼ cup of cilantro, chopped
- 3 tablespoons of low-fat plain yogurt
- 3 tablespoons of flour
- ¼ teaspoon of cumin
- ¼ teaspoon of turmeric
- ¼ teaspoon of ground coriander
- ¼ teaspoon of garam masala
- 1 small serrano chili, seeded and diced
- 2 cloves of garlic, minced
- ¼ cup of egg substitute
- ½ recipe of Coconut Curry Sauce

Directions:

1. Combine all ingredients and mix well.
2. Place meatballs on a sprayed sheet pan and bake for 7 minutes.
3. Place curry sauce in a saucepan over medium heat and bring to a simmer.
4. Coat cooked meatballs with curry sauce and serve over rice.

Nutrition:

- Calories: 246
- Carbs: 9g
- Fat: 10g
- Protein: 22g

27. Chicken, Tomato and Green Beans

- Serving Size: 4
- Preparation Time: 15 minutes
- Cooking Time: 25 minutes

Ingredients:

- 6 oz. low-sodium canned tomato paste
- 2 tbsp of Olive oil
- ¼ tsp of black pepper
- 2 lbs trimmed green beans
- 2 tbsp of Chopped parsley
- 1 ½ lb boneless, skinless and cubed chicken breasts
- 25 oz. no-salt-added canned tomato sauce

Directions:

1. Heat a pan with 50 % of the oil over medium heat, add chicken, stir, cover, cook within 5 minutes on both sides and transfer to a bowl.
2. Heat inside the same pan while using rest through the oil over medium heat, add green beans, stir and cook for 10 minutes.
3. Return chicken to that pan, add black pepper, tomato sauce, tomato paste and parsley, stir, cover and cook for 10 minutes more.
4. Divide between plates and serve. Enjoy!

Nutrition:

- Calories:217
- Carbs: 12g
- Fat: 4g
- Protein: 9g

28. Citrus Pork

- Serving Size: 4
- Preparation Time: 10 minutes
- Cooking Time: 30 minutes

Ingredients:

- Zest of 2 limes, grated
- Zest of 1 orange, grated
- Juice of 1 orange
- Juice of 2 limes
- 4 teaspoons garlic, minced
- ¾ cup of olive oil
- 1 cup of cilantro, chopped
- 1 cup of mint, chopped
- Black pepper to the taste
- 4 pork loin steaks

Directions:

1. In your food processor, mix lime zest and juice with orange zest and juice, garlic, oil, cilantro, mint and pepper and blend well.
2. Put the steaks in a bowl, add the citrus mix and toss really well.
3. Heat up a large-sized pan over medium-high heat, add pork steaks and the marinade and cook for 4 minutes on each side.
4. Put the pan in the oven and bake at 350 degrees F for 20 minutes.
5. Divide the steaks between plates, drizzle some of the cooking juices all over and serve with a side salad.
6. Enjoy!

Nutrition:

- Calories: 241
- Carbs: 8g
- Fat: 7g
- Protein: 20g

29. Green Bean Casserole

- Serving Size: 8
- Preparation Time: 15 minutes
- Cooking Time: 25 minutes

Ingredients:

- ½ yellow onion, sliced thin
- 2 tablespoons of butter
- 1 cup of breadcrumbs
- ½ cup of low-fat Parmesan cheese
- 1 cup of low-fat or fat-free cream of mushroom soup
- ½ cup of skim milk
- 1 teaspoon of soy sauce
- Fresh ground black pepper
- 4 cups of cut green beans, frozen and thawed
- 1 tablespoon of dry thyme

Directions:

1. Sauté onions in butter and add breadcrumbs and Parmesan.
2. Cover with breadcrumbs and onion mixture and bake for 20–25 minutes.
3. Divide between plates and serve. Enjoy!

Nutrition:

- Calories: 227
- Carbs: 20g
- Fat: 6g
- Protein: 6g

30. Nut-Crusted Chicken Breasts

- Serving Size: 4
- Preparation Time: 25 minutes
- Cooking Time: 20 minutes

Ingredients:

- 2 boneless, skinless chicken breasts, lightly pounded to even thickness
- ¼ cup of flour
- 3 ounces of liquid egg replacement
- Salt and pepper, to taste
- ¼ teaspoon of cinnamon
- ¼ teaspoon of dry thyme
- ¼ teaspoon of dry mustard
- 1/8 teaspoon of cayenne
- ½ cup of very finely chopped pistachios, walnuts, almonds, or pecans
- 2 tablespoons of canola oil
- 4 tablespoons of maple syrup
- 1 tablespoon of Dijon mustard

Directions:

1. Lightly dust chicken in flour and coat in beaten egg replacement.
2. In a medium bowl, combine salt and pepper, cinnamon, thyme, dry mustard and cayenne with the chopped nuts.
3. Dredge (dip) chicken into the nut mixture and press to completely cover the chicken. Place oil in a nonstick pan and heat over medium heat.
4. Place chicken in the pan and cook until nuts brown (2-3 minutes), flip and cook for 2-3 minutes on the second side, then place chicken in the oven for 5-7 minutes.
5. Pour over the chicken for the last 2 minutes in the oven.
6. Divide between plates and serve. Enjoy!

Nutrition:

- Calories: 320, Fat: 16g , Protein: 20g , Fiber: 2g

31. Roast Pork Loin with Rosemary and Garlic

- Serving Size: 8
- Preparation Time: 22 minutes
- Cooking Time: 45 minutes

Ingredients:

- 3 tablespoons of chopped rosemary
- 4 cloves of garlic, minced
- 1 teaspoon of kosher salt, divided
- ½ teaspoon of black pepper
- 1 (2-pound) boneless center-cut pork loin roast, visible fat trimmed
- 4 teaspoons of extra-virgin olive oil, divided

Directions:

1. In a small bowl, combine rosemary, garlic, salt and pepper.
2. Mix the pork with the rosemary mixture on the meat and bake for 30 minutes.
3. Serve.

Nutrition:

- Calories: 290
- Carbs: 1g
- Fat: 18g
- Protein: 30g

32. Chicken and Cheese Stuffed Peppers

- Serving Size: 6
- Preparation Time: 25 minutes
- Cooking Time: 55 minutes

Ingredients:

- 2 tbsp of olive oil
- 3 Tbsp of butter
- 4 bell peppers yellow
- 3 cloves of garlic, minced
- 1 large white onion chopped
- 2 lb. ground chicken
- 1 teaspoon of chili powder
- 10-ounce canned tomatoes chopped
- 1 1/2 cups of cheddar grated
- Black pepper and salt to taste
- 1 1/2 cups of mayonnaise
- 10 oz green leafy leaves

Directions:

1. Bake at 350 F. Slice the bell peppers in half in length and remove the seeds. Sprinkle in olive oil. In a saucepan and cook garlic and onions for three minutes. Mix in the chili powder, chicken salt and pepper. Cook for up to 8 minutes.
2. Mix in the tomatoes and sauté for another 3-4 minutes. Scoop the tomato mixture into the bell peppers. Then top with cheddar cheese and put it in a greased baking dish. Bake until cheese melts and becomes bubbly about 25-30 minutes.
3. Serve with mayonnaise and greens.

Nutrition:

- Calories: 335
- Carbs: 10g
- Fat: 57g
- Protein: 38g

33. Chicken Relleno Casserole

- Serving Size: 6
- Preparation Time: 19 minutes
- Cooking Time: 29 minutes

Ingredients:

- 6 Tortilla Factory low-carb whole wheat tortillas, torn into small pieces
- 1 ½ cups of hand-shredded cheese, Mexican
- 1 beaten egg
- 1 cup of milk
- 2 cups of cooked chicken, shredded
- 1 can Rotel
- ½ cup of salsa verde

Directions:

1. Grease an 8 x 8 glass baking dish
2. Heat oven to 375 degrees
3. Combine everything together, but reserve ½ cup of the cheese
4. Bake it for 29 minutes
5. Take it out of the oven and add ½ cup of cheese
6. Broil for about 2 minutes to melt the cheese
7. Divide between plates and serve. Enjoy!

Nutrition:

- Calories: 265, Carbs: 18g, Fat: 16g, Protein: 20g

34. Coconut Fried Shrimp with Cilantro Sauce

- Serving Size: 2
- Preparation Time: 10 minutes
- Cooking Time: 20 minutes

Ingredients:

- 2 teaspoons coconut flour
- 2 tbsp of grated Pecorino cheese
- 1 egg, beat in the bowl of
- 1/4 tsp of curry powder
- 1/2 lb shrimp, shelled
- 2 tablespoons coconut oil
- Add salt to the sauce
- 2 tbsp of Ghee
- 2 tbsp of cilantro leaves, chopped
- 1/2 onion, diced
- 1 cup of coconut cream
- 1/2 1 oz Paneer cheese grated

Directions:

1. Mix the flour, Pecorino and curry and salt in an ice-cold bowl. The coconut oil is melted in an oven over medium-high high heat.
2. Dip the shrimp into the egg that has been beaten, then coat them in this cheese mix. Grill until crispy and golden, around 5 minutes.
3. In a separate skillet, melt the Ghee. Cook the onion for three minutes. Mix in coconut milk and Paneer cheese. Cook until the sauce becomes thicker, approximately 3-4 minutes. Add the shrimp and toss thoroughly.
4. Serve warm with cilantro.

Nutrition:

- Calories: 341
- Carbs: 7.3g
- Fat: 54g
- Protein: 31g

35. Rosemary Braised Chicken with Mushroom Sauce

- Serving Size: 4
- Preparation Time: 15 minutes
- Cooking Time: 30 minutes

Ingredients:

- 1 pound of boneless skinless chicken thighs
- 2 tablespoons of canola oil
- 2 slices of turkey bacon or turkey prosciutto
- 1 small shallot, diced
- ¼ cup of yellow onion, diced
- 1 clove of garlic, crushed
- 3 sprigs of fresh rosemary
- 3 ounces of fresh cremini mushrooms, quartered
- 1 portobello mushroom cap, halved and sliced
- 1 teaspoon of flour
- 1 cup of low-sodium vegetable stock
- ½ cup of red wine
- Salt and pepper to taste

Directions:

1. Lightly coat chicken with oil, place in a deep-sided skillet over medium heat and brown on all sides (approximately 5 minutes per side).
2. Add bacon, shallots, onions, garlic, rosemary and mushrooms and sauté for 10 minutes.
3. Add flour, stock and red wine; cover and reduce liquid by half until thick and chicken is cooked (approximately 10 minutes).

Nutrition:

- Calories: 380
- Carbs: 9g
- Fat: 21g
- Protein: 33g

- Serving Size: 6
- Preparation Time: 15 mins
- Cooking Time: 45 minutes

Ingredients:

- 2 tbsp of olive oil
- 1 bell pepper, seeded and chopped
- 1 small onion, chopped
- 2 garlic cloves, finely chopped
- 1 lb. lean ground turkey
- 1 (15-oz.) can sugar-free pumpkin puree
- 1 (14-oz.) can dice tomatoes with liquid
- 1 tsp of ground cumin
- ½ tsp of ground turmeric
- ½ tsp of ground cinnamon
- 1¼ C. water
- 1 (18-oz.) can chickpeas, drained

Directions:

1. In a large-sized pan, heat oil over medium-low heat and sauté bell pepper, onion and garlic for about 5 minutes.
2. Add turkey and cook for about 5-6 minutes.
3. Add tomatoes, pumpkin, spices and water and cook until boiling over high heat.
4. Now adjust the heat to medium-low heat and stir in the chickpeas.
5. Simmer, covered for about 30 minutes, stirring occasionally.
6. Divide into portions and serve hot.

Nutrition:

- Calories: 317
- Carbs: 31g
- Fat: 11.6g
- Protein: 20.9g

37. Chicken Cacciatore

- Serving Size: 6
- Preparation Time: 5 minutes
- Cooking Time: 45 minutes

Ingredients:

- 2 tablespoons extra virgin olive oil
- 6 chicken thighs
- 1 sweet onion, chopped
- 2 garlic cloves, minced
- 2 red bell peppers, cored and diced
- 2 carrots, diced
- 1 rosemary sprig
- 1 thyme sprig
- 4 tomatoes, peeled and diced
- ½ cup of tomato juice
- ¼ cup of dry white wine
- 1 cup of chicken stock
- 1 bay leaf
- Salt and pepper to taste

Directions:

1. Heat the oil in a heavy sauce skillet.
2. Cook chicken on all sides until golden.
3. Add the mixture of garlic and onion and cook for 2 minutes.
4. Stir in the rest of the ingredients and season with salt and pepper.
5. Cook on low heat for 30 minutes.
6. Serve the chicken cacciatore warm and fresh.

Nutrition:

- Calories: 363
- Carbs: 7g
- Fat: 14g
- Protein: 42g

38. Coconut Chicken and Mushrooms

- Serving Size: 4
- Preparation Time: 10 minutes
- Cooking Time: 40 minutes

Ingredients:

- 2 tablespoons olive oil
- 1 yellow onion, chopped
- ½ pounds Bella mushrooms, sliced
- 2 pounds chicken thighs, boneless and skinless
- 3 carrots, sliced
- 2 celery stalks, chopped
- ½ cup of coconut cream
- 1 tablespoon of thyme, chopped
- 1 tablespoon of cilantro, chopped

Directions:

1. Heat up a pan with the oil over medium heat, add the onion, carrots and celery and sauté for 5 minutes.
2. Add the mushrooms and the meat and brown for 5 minutes more.
3. Add the rest of the ingredients, toss, cook over medium heat for 30 minutes more, divide between plates and serve.

Nutrition:

- Calories: 300
- Carbs: 15g
- Fat: 6g
- Protein: 16g

39. Chicken with Potatoes Olives and Sprouts

- Serving Size: 4
- Preparation Time: 15 minutes
- Cooking Time: 35 minutes

Ingredients:
- 1 pound chicken breasts, skinless, boneless and cut into pieces
- ¼ cup of olives, quartered
- 1 teaspoon of oregano
- 1 ½ teaspoon of Dijon mustard
- 1 lemon juice
- 1/3 cup of vinaigrette dressing
- 1 medium onion, diced
- 3 cups of potatoes cut into pieces
- 4 cups of Brussels sprouts, trimmed and quartered
- ¼ teaspoon of pepper
- ¼ teaspoon of salt

Directions:
1. Warm-up oven to 400 F. Place chicken in the center of the baking tray, then place potatoes, sprouts and onions around the chicken.
2. In a small bowl, mix vinaigrette, oregano, mustard, lemon juice and salt and pour over chicken and veggies. Sprinkle olives and season with pepper.
3. Bake in preheated oven for 20 minutes. Transfer chicken to a plate.
4. Stir the vegetables and roast for 15 minutes more.
5. Serve and enjoy.

Nutrition:
- Calories: 397
- Carbs: 31.4g
- Fat: 13g
- Protein: 38.3g

40. Cod Salad with Mustard

- Serving Size: 4
- Preparation Time: 12 minutes
- Cooking Time: 12 minutes

Ingredients:
- 4 medium cod fillets, skinless and boneless
- 2 tablespoons mustard
- 1 tablespoon of tarragon, chopped
- 1 tablespoon of capers, drained
- 4 tablespoons olive oil+ 1 teaspoon of
- Black pepper to the taste
- 2 cups of baby arugula
- 1 small red onion, sliced
- 1 small cucumber, sliced
- 2 tablespoons lemon juice

Directions:
1. In a bowl, mix mustard with 2 tablespoons olive oil, tarragon and capers and whisk.
2. Heat up a pan with 1 teaspoon of oil over medium-high heat, add fish, season with black pepper to the taste, cook for 6 minutes on each side and cut into medium cubes.
3. In a salad bowl, combine the arugula with onion, cucumber, lemon juice, cod and mustard mix, toss and serve.
4. Enjoy!

Nutrition:
- Calories: 258
- Carbs: 12g
- Fat: 12g
- Protein: 18g

41. Beef and Mushroom Meatloaf

- Serving Size: 4
- Preparation Time: 30 minutes
- Cooking Time: 1 hour 10 minutes

Ingredients:

- 1/2 lb ground beef
- 1/2 onion chopped
- 1 Tbsp of almond milk
- 1 tablespoon of almond flour
- 1 clove of garlic, minced
- 1 cup of chopped mushrooms
- 1 small egg
- Black pepper and salt to taste
- 1 Tbsp of chopped parsley, chopped
- 1/3 cup of Parmesan cheese, grated Glaze
- 1/3 cup of balsamic vinegar
- 1/4 tbsp of the xylitol
- 1/4 tbsp of tomato paste
- 1/4 teaspoon of garlic powder
- 1/4 teaspoon of onion powder
- 1 tbsp of ketchup Sugar-free

Directions:

1. Ensure to grease a loaf pan with cooking spray and then set it aside. Preheat the oven to 390 F.
2. Mix the meatloaf ingredients into one large bowl. Then, press the mixture into the loaf pan that you have prepared.
3. Bake the loaf in the oven for around 30 minutes.
4. For the glaze, mix all the ingredients in the bowl.
5. Drizzle the glaze onto the meatloaf. Return the meatloaf to the oven for another 20 minutes.
6. Let meatloaf sit for 10 minutes before slicing. Serve and have fun!

Nutrition:

- Calories: 311, Carbs: 5.5g, Fat: 21g, Protein: 24g

42. Chicken and Sausage Gumbo

- Serving Size: 4
- Preparation Time: 25 minutes
- Cooking Time: 40 minutes

Ingredients:

- 1 sausage, sliced
- 2 chicken breasts cubed
- 1 stick of celery chopped
- 1 leaf of a bay
- 1 bell pepper cut into pieces
- 1 onion chopped
- 1 cup of chopped tomatoes, 1
- 4 cups of chicken broth
- 2 tbsp of garlic powder
- 2 1 tbsp of dry mustard
- 1 2 tbsp of chili powder
- Black pepper and salt to taste
- 2 tbsp of Cajun seasoning
- 3 tbsp of olive oil
- 1 tablespoon of sage cut into pieces

Directions:

1. The olive oil is heated in an oven at medium temperature. Add the chicken and sausage and cook for five minutes.
2. Add the other ingredients, except the sage and bring to the boiling point. Simmer for 25 minutes.
3. Serve with sage sprinkled.

Nutrition:

- Calories: 303
- Carbs: 8.7g
- Fat: 23g
- Protein: 36g

43. Feta and Mozzarella Chicken

- Serving Size: 4
- Preparation Time: 25 minutes
- Cooking Time: 45 minutes

Ingredients:

- 1.25 lbs chicken breasts chopped
- 1/2 teaspoon of mixed spice seasoning
- Black pepper and salt to taste
- 1 cup of baby spinach
- 2 tsp of olive oil
- 4 oz feta cheese, crumbled
- 1/2 cup of mozzarella, shredded

Directions:

1. Rub the chicken with the spice mix, salt and black pepper. Place it into a baking dish, then place the spinach on top. Blend the olive oil, mozzarella cheese and feta, as well as 1 cup of water and black pepper. Stir.
2. Sprinkle the mix over the chicken and then put the casserole on aluminum foil. Bake to cook for about 20 minutes. 350 F, remove the foil and cook for 15 minutes or until a nice golden-brown color has formed over the top. Serve.

Nutrition:

- Calories: 343
- Carbs: 3.2g
- Fat: 20g
- Protein: 32g

44. Steak Fajitas

- Serving Size: 8
- Preparation Time: 5 minutes
- Cooking Time: 25 minutes

Ingredients:

- 1 onion cut into strips
- 1 green bell cut into strips
- ½ teaspoon of thyme
- ½ teaspoon of mustard powder
- 1 teaspoon of black pepper
- 1 teaspoon of cumin
- 2 teaspoons of dried rosemary
- 2 teaspoons of chili powder
- 2 packets of natural sweetener
- 1 tablespoon of paprika
- 1 tablespoon of sea salt
- 1 pound of lean sirloin steak, cut into strips

Directions:

1. Place the salt, paprika, sweetener, chili powder, dried rosemary, cumin, pepper, mustard powder and dried thyme into a bowl and mix well to actually combine.
2. Take out one tsp of this mixture and reserve.
3. Place a large skillet on the stove and heat to medium-high.
4. Add the prepared onion and pepper to the skillet along with the spice mixture that you set to the side earlier. You need to cook the onion and peppers until they have softened up and the onions turn translucent.
5. Take off the heat and place in a bowl. Cover to keep warm.
6. Into the same skillet, add half the seasoned steak and cook for about two minutes per side or until done to your liking. Place cooked steak onto a clean plate and cover until the rest of the steak gets done.
7. Once all the steak strips are done, add everything back into the skillet and warm everything up for a few minutes.
8. Spoon onto plates and enjoy.

Nutrition: Calories: 401, Carbs: 6g, Fat: 22.1g, Protein: 104.7g

- Serving Size: 6
- Preparation Time: 20 minutes
- Cooking Time: 40 minutes

Ingredients:

- 6 ounces of dried wide whole wheat egg noodles
- 2 teaspoons of canola oil
- ½ cup of softened, chopped sun-dried tomatoes, not oil-packed
- 1 small onion, diced small
- 1 red bell pepper, diced small
- 1 clove of minced garlic
- 1 stalk of celery, diced
- 2 tablespoons of all-purpose flour
- 2 cups of skim milk
- ½ cup of fat-free mayonnaise
- 1 can of spring water-packed tuna, drained (or canned chicken)
- ½ cup of grated low-fat Swiss cheese
- 2 tablespoons of chopped fresh basil
- 1 tablespoon of lemon juice
- Salt and pepper, to taste
- 1/3 cup of toasted almonds

Directions:

1. Preheat oven to 425°F.
2. Cook pasta for about 6 minutes, drain, rinse in cold water and set aside.
3. Heat the pan and add oil and garlic. Cook vegetables and tomatoes for 3 minutes then add the milk and flour and cook for 4 minutes.
4. Stir in mayo, tuna, cheese and basil.
5. Season with lemon juice, salt and pepper.
6. Sprinkle with almonds and bake for 20 minutes.
7. Let stand 5 minutes before serving.

Nutrition:

- Calories: 310, Carbs: 37g, Fat: 9g, Protein: 23g

DINNER RECIPES

46. Balsamic Chili Roast

- Serving Size: 6
- Preparation Time: 10 minutes
- Cooking Time: 4 hours

Ingredients:

- 4-pound pork roast
- 6 garlic cloves, minced
- 1 yellow onion, chopped
- ½ cup of balsamic vinegar
- 1 cup of low-sodium chicken stock
- 2 tablespoons coconut aminos
- Black pepper to the taste
- A pinch of red chili pepper flakes

Directions:

1. Put the roast in a baking dish, add garlic, onion, vinegar, stock, aminos, black pepper and chili flakes, cover, introduce in the oven and cook at 325 degrees F for 4 hours.
2. Slice, divide between plates and serve with a side salad.
3. Enjoy!

Nutrition:

- Calories: 265
- Carbs: 15g
- Fat: 7g
- Protein: 32g

47. Beef and Bell Pepper Frittata

- Serving Size: 4
- Preparation Time: 30 minutes
- Cooking Time: 55 minutes

Ingredients:

- 1 tbsp of butter
- 12 OZ ground sausage made from beef
- 1/4 cup of shredded cheddar
- 12 whole eggs
- 1 cup of sour cream
- 2 bell peppers red cut into pieces
- Black pepper and salt to taste

Directions:

1. Preheat the oven to 350 F. Crack eggs in a blender. Add the salt, sour cream and pepper. Then, at a low speed, blend the ingredients. Set aside.
2. In a large skillet at medium-high temperature. Add bell peppers and cook until soft, 6 mins to put aside. Add the beef sausage and cook until golden brown, continually stirring and breaking the lumps into tiny pieces for 10 minutes.
3. The beef is then flattened on the bottom of the skillet. Sprinkle bell peppers on top, pour the egg mixture all over and sprinkle top cheddar cheese. Place the skillet in the oven for at least 30 mins or so until the eggs are set and the cheese melts.
4. Take the frittata out, cut it into slices and serve warm with salad.

Nutrition:

- Calories: 321
- Carbs: 6.5g
- Fat: 49g
- Protein: 33g

48. Brown Basmati Rice Pilaf

- Serving Size: 2
- Preparation Time: 10 minutes
- Cooking Time: 3 minutes

Ingredients:

- ½ tablespoon of vegan butter
- ½ cup of mushrooms, chopped
- ½ cup of brown basmati rice
- 2-3 tablespoons water
- 1/8 teaspoon of dried thyme
- Ground pepper to taste
- ½ tablespoon of olive oil
- ¼ cup of green onion, chopped
- 1 cup of vegetable broth
- ¼ teaspoon of salt
- ¼ cup of chopped, toasted pecans

Directions:

1. Place a saucepan over medium-low heat. Add butter and oil.
2. When it melts, add mushrooms and cook until slightly tender.
3. Stir in the green onion and brown rice. Cook for 3 minutes. Stir constantly.
4. Stir in the broth, water, salt and thyme.
5. When it begins to boil, lower the heat and cover with a lid. Simmer until rice is cooked. Add more water or broth if required.
6. Stir in the pecans and pepper.
7. Serve.

Nutrition:

- Calories: 189, Carbs: 19g , Fats: 11g , Proteins: 4g

49. Cabbage and Beef Steaks

- Serving Size: 4
- Preparation Time: 25 minutes
- Cooking Time: 55 minutes

Ingredients:
- 1 lb. chuck steak
- 1 headcanon cabbage, grated
- 1/4 cup of olive oil
- 3 tablespoons coconut flour
- 1 tsp of Italian mixed herb blend
- 1 cup of bone broth

Directions:
1. Preheat the oven to a heat of 380 F. Cut the steak into thin strips across the grain using an abrasive knife. Put the coconut flour and the steak slices in a zipper bag. Close the bag and shake it to coat. Create little mounds of cabbage in a well-greased baking dish.
2. Remove the meat strips made of coconut flour. Shake off any excess flour and place 3-4 beef strips on each cabbage mound. Sprinkle with the Italian herb mix and drizzle it with the olive oil remaining. Roast for about 30 minutes.
3. Take the pan off and add the broth. Place back in the oven and cook for another 10 minutes, or until the meat is cooked.
4. Serve and enjoy!

Nutrition:
- Calories: 331
- Carbs: 4.5g
- Fat: 20g
- Protein: 23g

50. Chicken and Chorizo Traybake

- Serving Size: 4
- Preparation Time: 10 minutes
- Cooking Time: 50 minutes

Ingredients:

- 1 bell pepper red broken into pieces
- 1/2 cup of mushrooms, chopped
- 1 lb chorizo sausages, sliced
- 4 tbsp of olive oil
- 1 teaspoon of dried rosemary
- 4 cherry peppers cut into pieces
- 1 red onion Cut into wedges
- 2 garlic cloves, chopped
- 2 cups of tomatoes cut into pieces
- 1 lb of chicken thighs
- Black pepper and salt to taste
- 1/2 cup of chicken stock
- 2 tbsp of capers
- 1 tbsp of chopped parsley

Directions:

1. Set the oven temperature up to 390 F. In a small bowl, mix your garlic, two tablespoons of olive oil, dried rosemary, salt and pepper. Stir it until the ingredients are well blended. Rub the mixture on the chicken.
2. On a baking tray, mix the bell pepper, mushrooms, chorizo, red onions, capers, cherry peppers, tomatoes, and the remaining olive oil, salt and pepper. Lay the chicken thighs skin-side up on top of each other, then pour them into the chicken broth. Roast for 40-50 minutes, or until the skin of the chicken is crisp and the veggies have been softened.
3. Add parsley to the chicken and enjoy the warmth.

Nutrition:

- Calories: 305
- Carbs: 8.3g
- Fat: 56g
- Protein: 42g

51. Chicken Tikka

- Serving Size: 6
- Preparation Time: 15 minutes
- Cooking Time: 20 minutes

Ingredients:

- 4 chicken breasts, skinless, boneless; cubed
- 2 large onions, cubed
- 10 Cherry tomatoes
- 1/3 cup of plain non-fat yogurt
- 4 garlic cloves, crushed
- 1 ½ inch fresh ginger, peeled and chopped
- 1 small onion, grated
- 1 ½ teaspoons of chili powder
- 1 Tablespoon of ground coriander
- 1 teaspoon of salt
- 2 tablespoons of coriander leaves

Directions:

1. In a large bowl, combine the non-fat yogurt, crushed garlic, ginger, chili powder, coriander, salt and pepper. Add the cubed chicken and stir until the chicken is coated. Cover with plastic film and place in the fridge. Marinate for 2 – 4 hours.
2. After marinating the chicken, get some skewers ready. Alternate pieces of chicken cubes, cherry tomatoes and cubed onions onto the skewers.
3. Grill within 6 – 8 minutes on each side. Once the chicken is cooked through, pull the meat and vegetables off the skewers onto plates. Garnish with coriander. Serve immediately.

Nutrition:

- Calories: 417, Carbs: 59g, Fat: 19g, Protein: 19g

52. Chicken with Garlic and Fennel

- Serving Size: 4
- Preparation Time: 10 minutes
- Cooking Time: 45 minutes

Ingredients:

- 2 yellow onions, chopped
- 2 pounds of chicken breast, skinless, boneless and roughly cubed
- 2 fennel bulbs, shredded
- 4 garlic cloves, minced
- 2 tablespoons olive oil
- 1 cup of chicken stock
- A pinch of sea salt and black pepper
- 2 tablespoons parsley, chopped

Directions:

1. Heat up a pan with the oil over medium heat, add the onions and the garlic and sauté for 5 minutes.
2. Add the fennel and the meat and brown for 5 minutes more.
3. Add the rest of the ingredients, toss, bring to a simmer and cook over medium heat for 35 minutes.
4. Divide everything between plates and serve.

Nutrition:

- Calories: 200
- Carbs: 10g
- Fat: 4g
- Protein: 16g

53. Creamy Chicken Fried Rice

- Serving Size: 4
- Preparation Time: 15 minutes
- Cooking Time: 45 minutes

Ingredients:

- 2 pounds of chicken; white and dark meat (diced into cubes)
- 2 Tablespoons butter or margarine
- 1 ½ cups of instant rice
- 1 cup of mixed frozen vegetables
- 1 can condensed cream of chicken soup
- 1 cup of water
- 1 cube instant chicken bouillon
- Salt and pepper to taste

Directions:

1. Take the vegetables out of the freezer. Set aside. Warm a large, deep skillet over medium heat, add the butter or margarine. Place the chicken in the skillet, season with salt and pepper. Fry until both sides are brown.
2. Remove the chicken, then adjust the heat and add the rice. Add the water and bouillon. Cook the rice, then add the chicken, the vegetables. Mix in the soup, then simmer until the vegetables are tender.
3. Serve immediately.

Nutrition:

- Calories: 319, Carbs: 63g, Fat: 18g, Protein: 22g

54. Mixed Grains Chili

- Serving Size: 12
- Preparation Time: 15 minutes
- Cooking Time: 55 minutes

Ingredients:

- 2 tbsp of olive oil
- 2 shallots, chopped
- 1 large yellow onion, chopped
- 1 tbsp of fresh ginger root, finely grated
- 8 garlic cloves, minced
- 1 tsp of ground cumin
- 3 tbsp of red chili powder
- Salt and ground black pepper, as required
- 1 (28-oz.) can crushed tomatoes
- 1 canned chipotle pepper, mince
- 1 Serrano pepper, seeded and finely chopped
- 2/3 cup of bulgur wheat
- 2/3 cups of pearl barley
- 2¼ cups of mixed lentils (green, black, brown), rinsed
- 1½ cups of canned chickpeas
- 3 scallions, chopped

Directions:

1. In a large-sized Dutch oven, heat oil over medium heat and sauté shallot and onion for about 4-5 minutes.
2. Add ginger, garlic, cumin and chili powder and sauté for about 1 minute.
3. Stir in tomatoes, both peppers and broth. Stir in the remaining ingredients except the scallion and bring to a rolling boil.
4. Immediately adjust the heat to low and simmer for about 35-45 minutes or until the desired thickness of the chili.
5. Serve hot with the topping of scallion.

Nutrition:

- Calories: 311, Carbs: 61g, Fat: 4.9g, Protein: 18.6g

55. Cumin Pork and Beans

- Serving Size: 4
- Preparation Time: 10 minutes
- Cooking Time: 1 hour

Ingredients:

- 2 pounds of pork stew meat, roughly cubed
- 1 cup of canned pinto beans
- 4 scallions, chopped
- 2 tablespoons olive oil
- 1 tablespoon of chili powder
- 2 teaspoons cumin, ground
- A pinch of salt and black pepper
- 2 garlic cloves, minced
- 1 cup of vegetable stock
- A handful of parsley, chopped

Directions:

1. Heat up a pan with the oil over medium-high heat, add the scallions and the garlic and sauté for 5 minutes.
2. Add the meat and brown for approximately about 5 minutes more.
3. Add the beans and the other ingredients, toss, introduce the pan to the oven and cook everything at 380 degrees F for 50 minutes.
4. Divide the mix between plates and serve.

Nutrition:

- Calories: 291
- Carbs: 15g
- Fat: 4g
- Protein: 24g

56. Beef & Mushroom Soup

- Serving Size: 8
- Preparation Time: 15 minutes
- Cooking Time: 20 minutes

Ingredients:

- 8 cups of homemade chicken broth
- 2-3 cups of broccoli, chopped
- 8 oz. of fresh mushrooms, sliced
- 1 bunch of scallion, chopped (reserve dark green part for garnishing)
- 1 (1-inch) piece of fresh ginger root, minced
- 4 garlic cloves, minced
- 1½ lb. of cooked beef meat, thinly sliced
- ½ tsp of red pepper flakes, crushed
- 3 tbsp of coconut aminos

Directions:

1. In a soup pan, add broth and bring to a rolling boil.
2. Stir in broccoli pieces and cook for about 1-2 minutes.
3. Stir in mushroom, scallions, ginger and garlic and simmer for about 7-8 minutes.
4. Stir in beef, red pepper flakes and coconut aminos and adjust the heat to low. Simmer for about 3-5 minutes.
5. Serve hot with the garnishing of the reserved green part of the scallion.

Nutrition:

- Calories: 305
- Carbs: 5.9g
- Fat: 6.9g
- Protein: 32.5g

57. Chicken & Spinach Stew

- Serving Size: 5
- Preparation Time: 15 mins
- Cooking Time: 35 minutes

Ingredients:

- 2 tbsp of extra-virgin olive oil
- 1 yellow onion, chopped
- 1 tbsp of garlic, minced
- 1 tbsp of fresh ginger root, minced
- 1 tsp of ground turmeric
- 1 tsp of ground cumin
- 1 tsp of ground coriander
- 1 tsp of paprika
- 4 (4-oz.) boneless, skinless chicken thighs, cut into 1-inch pieces
- 4 tomatoes, chopped
- 14 oz. unsweetened coconut milk
- Salt and ground black pepper, as required
- 6 C. fresh spinach, chopped
- 2 tbsp of fresh lemon juice

Directions:

1. Heat oil in a large-sized heavy-bottomed pan over medium heat and sauté the onion for about 3-4 minutes.
2. Add the ginger, garlic and spices and sauté for about 1 minute.
3. Add the chicken and cook for about 4-5 minutes.
4. Add the tomatoes, coconut milk, salt and black pepper and bring to a gentle simmer.
5. Now, adjust the heat to low and simmer, covered for about 10-15 minutes.
6. Stir in the spinach and cook for about 4-5 minutes.
7. Add lemon juice and remove from heat.
8. Serve hot.

Nutrition:

- Calories: 227, Carbs: 9.44g, Fat: 14.3g, Protein: 28.7g

58. Beans & Lentil Soup

- Serving Size: 6
- Preparation Time: 15 minutes
- Cooking Time: 40 minutes

Ingredients:

- 1 tbsp of olive oil
- 2 garlic cloves, minced
- 2 carrots, peeled and finely chopped
- 1 yellow onion, finely chopped
- 1 cup of dried lentils
- 1 (15-oz.) can of diced tomatoes
- 1 (15½-oz.) can of black beans, drained and rinsed
- ¾-1 tsp of chili powder
- ½ tsp of ground cumin
- ½ tsp of red pepper flakes, crushed
- Salt and ground black pepper, as required
- 4 C. homemade vegetable broth

Directions:

1. In a large-sized pan, heat the oil over medium heat and sauté garlic for about 1 minute.
2. Add the carrots and onion and sauté for about 5 minutes.
3. Stir in the remaining ingredients and bring to a rolling boil.
4. Adjust the heat to low and simmer, covered for about 25-30 minutes, stirring occasionally.
5. Serve hot.

Nutrition: Calories: 216, Carbs: 44g, Fat: 4.3g, Protein: 18.9g

59. Meatballs Curry

- Serving Size: 6
- Preparation Time: 20 minutes
- Cooking Time: 22 minutes

Ingredients:

For Meatballs

- 1 lb. of grass-fed lean ground beef
- 2 organic eggs, beaten
- 3 tbsp of red onion, minced
- ¼ C. fresh basil leaves, chopped
- 1 (1-inch) fresh ginger piece, finely chopped
- 4 garlic cloves, finely chopped
- 3 Serrano peppers, minced
- 1 tsp of coconut sugar
- 1 tbsp of red curry paste
- Salt, as required
- 1 tbsp of red boat fish sauce
- 2 tbsp of coconut oil

For Curry

- 1 red onion, chopped
- Salt, as required
- 4 garlic cloves, minced
- 1 (1-inch) fresh ginger piece, minced
- 2 Serrano peppers, minced
- 2 tbsp of red curry paste
- 1 (14-oz.) unsweetened coconut milk
- Salt and ground black pepper, as required

Directions:

1. For meatballs: in a large-sized bowl, add all ingredients except for oil and mix until well combined.
2. Make small-sized balls from the mixture.
3. In a large-sized wok, melt coconut oil over medium heat and cook meatballs for about 3-5 minutes or until golden brown from all sides.
4. Transfer the meatballs to a bowl.
5. In the same wok, add onion and a pinch of salt and sauté for about 5 minutes.
6. Add garlic, ginger and chilies and sauté for about 1 minute.
7. Add curry paste and sauté for about 1 minute.
8. Add coconut milk and meatballs and bring to a gentle simmer.
9. Reduce the heat to low and simmer, covered for about 10 minutes.
10. Serve hot.

Nutrition:

- Calories: 236, Carbs: 6.8g, Fat: 14.9g, Protein: 18g

- Serving Size: 6
- Preparation Time: 15 minutes
- Cooking Time: 15 minutes

Ingredients:

- 2 tsp of coconut oil, divided
- ½ cup of onion, thinly sliced
- 1½ lb. of shrimp, peeled and deveined
- ½ of red bell pepper, seeded and thinly sliced
- 1 mango, peeled, pitted and sliced
- 8 oz. can of pineapple tidbits with unsweetened juice
- 1 cup of unsweetened coconut milk
- 1 tbsp of red curry paste
- 2 tbsp of red boat fish sauce
- 2 tbsp of fresh cilantro, chopped

Directions:

1. In a non-stick pan, melt 1 tsp of coconut oil over medium-high heat and sauté onion for about 3-4 minutes.
2. With a spoon, push the onion to the side of the pan.
3. Add the remaining coconut oil and shrimp and cook for about 2 minutes per side.
4. Add bell pepper and cook for about 3-4 minutes.
5. Add remaining ingredients except for cilantro and simmer for about 5 minutes.
6. Serve hot with a sprinkling of cilantro.

Nutrition:

- Calories: 262
- Carbs: 19.7g
- Fat: 14g
- Protein: 27.9g

61. Healthy Vegetable Soup

- Serving Size: 4
- Preparation Time: 10 minutes
- Cooking Time: 15 minutes

Ingredients:
- 1 cup of tomatoes, chopped
- 1 small zucchini, diced
- 3 oz kale, sliced
- 1 tbsp of garlic, chopped
- 5 button mushrooms, sliced
- 2 carrots, peeled and sliced
- 2 celery sticks, sliced
- 1/2 red chili, sliced
- 1 onion, diced
- 1 tbsp of olive oil
- 1 bay leaf
- 4 cups of vegetable stock
- 1/4 tsp of salt

Directions:
1. Add oil into the inner pot of the instant pot and set the pot on sauté mode.
2. Add carrots, celery, onion and salt and cook for 2-3 minutes.
3. Add mushrooms and chili and cook for 2 minutes.
4. Add the remaining ingredients and stir everything well.
5. Seal the pot with a lid and cook on high for 10 minutes.
6. Once done, allow to release pressure naturally for 10 minutes then release the remaining using quick release. Remove lid.
7. Stir well and serve.

Nutrition:
- Calories: 100
- Carbs: 15.1g
- Fat: 3.8g
- Protein: 3.5g

- Serving Size: 4
- Preparation Time: 10 minutes
- Cooking Time: 15 minutes

Ingredients:

- 1/2 lb of ground pork
- 1 tbsp of fresh lemon juice
- 1/4 cup of fresh parsley, chopped
- 1 cup of water
- 14 oz can of tomatoes, chopped
- 2 cups of a can of navy beans, rinsed and drained
- 3 medium potatoes, peeled and diced
- 1 tbsp of garlic, chopped
- 1/2 tsp of red pepper flakes
- 1 tsp of dried thyme
- 1 carrot, peeled and diced
- 2 celery sticks, diced
- 1 onion, diced
- 2 tbsp of olive oil
- 2 tsp of salt

Directions:

1. Add oil into the inner pot of the instant pot and set the pot on sauté mode. Add carrot, celery, onion and 1 tsp of salt and sauté for 5 minutes.
2. Add meat and cook for 2-4 minutes.
3. Add remaining ingredients except for lemon juice and parsley and stir everything well. Seal the pot with a lid and cook on high for 6 minutes.
4. Once done, allow to release pressure naturally for 10 minutes then release the remaining using quick release. Remove lid.
5. Add lemon juice and stir well.
6. Garnish with parsley and serve.

Nutrition:

- Calories: 446, Carbs: 62.6g, Fat: 9.9g, Protein: 29.1g

63. Mixed Lentil Stew

- Serving Size: 4
- Preparation Time: 10 minutes
- Cooking Time: 30 minutes

Ingredients:

- 1 1/2 cups of mixed lentils, rinsed
- 1/4 cup of fresh cilantro, chopped
- 12 oz can of chickpeas, drained and rinsed
- 1 tsp of dried oregano
- 1 tsp of ground sumac
- 1 tsp of ground ginger
- 1 tsp of garlic powder
- 1 tbsp of ground cumin
- 1 tbsp of paprika
- 28 oz can of tomatoes, diced
- 2 zucchini, chopped
- 1 bell pepper, chopped
- 3 carrots, chopped
- 1 sweet potato, chopped
- 1 onion, chopped
- 4 1/2 cups of vegetable broth
- Pepper and salt to taste

Directions:

1. Add all ingredients except chickpeas and cilantro into the inner pot of the instant pot and stir well.
2. Seal the pot with a lid and cook on high for minutes.
3. Once done, release pressure using quick release. Remove lid. Add cilantro and chickpeas and stir well.
4. Serve and enjoy.

Nutrition:

- Calories: 523, Carbs: 102.6g, Fat: 4.2g, Protein: 22.5g

64. Spinach Chicken Stew

- Serving Size: 4
- Preparation Time: 10 minutes
- Cooking Time: 25 minutes

Ingredients:

- 2 cups of spinach, chopped
- 1 lb of chicken breasts, skinless, boneless and cut into chunks
- 1/2 cup of a can of tomato, crushed
- 1 cup of chicken stock
- 1 onion, chopped
- 1 tbsp of olive oil
- Pepper and salt to taste

Directions:

1. Add oil into the inner pot of the instant pot and set the pot on sauté mode. Add chicken and onion and sauté for 5 minutes.
2. Add remaining ingredients and stir well. Seal the pot with a lid and cook on low for 20 minutes.
3. Once done, allow to release pressure naturally for 10 minutes then release the remaining using quick release. Remove lid.
4. Stir well and serve.

Nutrition:

- Calories: 266
- Carbs: 4.2g
- Fat: 12.2 g
- Protein: 33.9g

65. Lamb Stew

- Serving Size: 4
- Preparation Time: 10 minutes
- Cooking Time: 25 minutes

Ingredients:

- 1 3/4 lbs of lamb shoulder, cut into chunks
- 1/4 cup of fresh parsley, chopped
- 1 tsp of dried basil
- 3/4 tsp of dried oregano
- 1 tbsp of olive oil
- 1/2 cup of onion, chopped
- 14 oz can tomatoes, chopped
- 1 tbsp of garlic, minced
- 1/4 cup of chicken broth
- Pepper and salt to taste

Directions:

1. Add oil into the inner pot of the instant pot and set the pot on sauté mode.
2. Add meat, garlic and onion and sauté for 5 minutes.
3. Add the remaining ingredients except for the parsley and stir well.
4. Seal the pot with a lid and cook on high pressure 20 for minutes.
5. Once done, release pressure using quick release. Remove lid.
6. Garnish with parsley and serve.

Nutrition:

- Calories: 434, Carbs: 7.6g, Fat: 18.2g, Protein: 57.4g

66. Easy & Delicious Beef Stew

- Serving Size: 4
- Preparation Time: 10 minutes
- Cooking Time: 30 minutes

Ingredients:

- 1 1/2 lbs of beef stew meat, cut into cubed
- 1/2 cup of sweet corn
- 1 cup a can of tomato, crushed
- 1 cup of chicken stock
- 4 carrots, chopped
- 1 onion, chopped
- 1 tbsp of olive oil
- Pepper and salt to taste

Directions:

1. Add oil into the inner pot of the instant pot and set the pot on sauté mode.
2. Add onion and meat and sauté for 5 minutes.
3. Add remaining ingredients and stir well.
4. Seal the pot with a lid and cook on high pressure 25 for minutes.
5. Once done, allow to release pressure naturally for 10 minutes then release the remaining using quick release. Remove lid.
6. Stir and serve.

Nutrition:

- Calories: 410, Carbs: 14g, Fat: 14.4g, Protein: 54.4g

67. Tomato Chickpeas Stew

- Serving Size: 4
- Preparation Time: 10 minutes
- Cooking Time: 25 minutes

Ingredients:

- 1 lb can of chickpeas, rinsed and drained
- 18 oz can tomatoes, chopped
- 1/2 tsp of red pepper flakes
- 2 tbsp of olive oil
- 1 tsp of dried oregano
- 1 tsp of garlic, minced
- 1 onion, chopped
- Pepper
- Salt

Directions:

1. Add oil into the inner pot of the instant pot and set the pot on sauté mode.
2. Add onion and garlic and sauté for 5 minutes.
3. Add remaining ingredients and stir well.
4. Seal the pot with a lid and cook on high pressure 20 for minutes.
5. Once done, allow to release pressure naturally for 10 minutes then release the remaining using quick release. Remove lid.
6. Serve and enjoy.

Nutrition:

- Calories 236
- Carbs: 35.3g
- Fat: 8.4g
- Protein: 7.2g

68. Chicken Lentil Stew

- Serving Size: 6
- Preparation Time: 10 minutes
- Cooking Time: 25 minutes

Ingredients:

- 2 lbs chicken thighs, boneless & skinless
- 1 tbsp of olive oil
- 1 cup of onion, chopped
- 4 cups of chicken stock
- 8 oz green lentils, soak for 1 hour
- 28 oz can tomato, diced
- Pepper
- Salt

Directions:

1. Add oil into the inner pot of the instant pot and set the pot on sauté mode.
2. Add onion and sauté for 5 minutes.
3. Add the rest of the ingredients and stir well.
4. Seal the pot with a lid and cook on high for minutes.
5. Once done, release pressure using quick release. Remove lid.
6. Shred chicken using a fork.
7. Stir well and serve.

Nutrition:

- Calories 479
- Carbs: 29.8g
- Fat: 14.3g
- Protein: 55.1g

69. Garlic Squash Broccoli Soup

- Serving Size: 4
- Preparation Time: 10 minutes
- Cooking Time: 15 minutes

Ingredients:

- 1 lb butternut squash, peeled and diced
- 1 lb broccoli florets
- 1 tsp of dried basil
- 1 tsp of paprika
- 2 1/2 cups of vegetable stock
- 1 tsp of garlic, minced
- 1 tbsp of olive oil
- 1 onion, chopped
- Salt to taste

Directions:

1. Add oil into the inner pot of the instant pot and set the pot on sauté mode.
2. Add onion and garlic and sauté for 3 minutes.
3. Add remaining ingredients and stir well.
4. Seal pot with lid and cook on high pressure 12 for minutes.
5. Once done, allow to release pressure naturally for 10 minutes then release the remaining using quick release. Remove lid.
6. Blend soup using an immersion blender until smooth.
7. Serve and enjoy.

Nutrition: Calories 137, Carb: 24.5g, Fat: 4.1g, Protein: 5g

70. Bean Soup

- Serving Size: 4
- Preparation Time: 15 minutes
- Cooking Time: 5 hours

Ingredients

- ½ cup of pinto beans, dried
- ½ bay leaf
- 1 garlic clove
- ½ white onion
- 2 cups of water
- 2 tbsp of cilantro, chopped
- 1 avocado, cubed
- ⅛ cup of white onion, chopped
- ¼ cup of Roma tomatoes, chopped
- 2 tbsp of chipotle pepper sauce
- ¼ tsp of kosher salt
- 2 tbsp of cilantro, chopped
- 2 tbsp of low-fat Monterrey Jack cheese, shredded

Directions

1. Place water, salt, onion, pepper, garlic, bay leaf and beans in the slow cooker.
2. Cook on high for 5-6 hours. Discard the Bay leaf.
3. Serve in heated bowls.

Nutrition

- Calories: 402, Carbs: 43g, Protein: 13g

71. Butternut Squash Soup

- Servings Size: 6
- Preparation Time: 15 minutes
- Cooking Time: 8 hours

Ingredients

- 1 butternut squash, peeled, seeded and diced
- 1 onion, chopped
- 1 sweet-tart apple peeled, cored and chopped
- 3 cups of vegetable broth or store-bought
- 1 tsp of garlic powder
- ½ tsp of sage, ground
- ¼ tsp of sea salt
- ¼ tsp of black pepper, freshly ground
- Pinch cayenne pepper
- Pinch nutmeg
- ½ cup of fat-free half-and-half

Directions

1. In your slow cooker, combine the squash, onion, apple, broth, garlic powder, sage, salt, black pepper, cayenne and nutmeg. Cook on low for 8 hours.
2. Using an immersion blender, countertop blender, or food processor, purée the soup, adding the half-and-half as you do.
3. Stir to combine and serve.

Nutrition

- Calories: 215
- Carbs: 5g
- Protein: 3g

72. Chickpea and Kale Soup

- Servings Size: 6
- Preparation Time: 15 minutes
- Cooking Time: 9 hours

Ingredients

- 1 summer squash, quartered lengthwise and sliced crosswise
- 1 zucchini, quartered lengthwise and sliced crosswise
- 2 cups of chickpeas, cooked and rinsed
- 1 cup of quinoa, uncooked
- 2 cans tomatoes, diced: with their juice
- 5 cups of vegetable broth, poultry broth, or store-bought
- 1 tsp of garlic powder
- 1 tsp of onion powder
- 1 tsp of thyme, dried
- ½ tsp of sea salt
- 2 cups of kale leaves, chopped

Directions

1. In your slow cooker, combine the summer squash, zucchini, chickpeas, quinoa, tomatoes (with their juice), broth, garlic powder, onion powder, thyme and salt.
2. Cover and cook on low for 8 hours. Stir in the kale.
3. Cover and cook on low for 1 more hour.
4. Serve.

Nutrition

- Calories: 350
- Carbs: 54g
- Fat: 9g
- Protein: 19g

73. Coconut Carrot Ginger Soup

- Serving Size: 6 to 8
- Preparation Time: 10 minutes
- Cooking Time: 30 minutes

Ingredients:

- 8 carrots, peeled and roughly chopped
- 1½-inch piece fresh ginger, sliced thin
- 1 large onion, peeled and roughly chopped
- 1¼ tsp of salt
- 2 cups of unsweetened coconut milk
- 4½ cups of plus 2 tbsp of water, divided

Directions:

1. Add the onion and 2 tablespoons of water to a large pot and sauté over medium heat for about 5 minutes, or until soft.
2. Place the carrots, the remaining 4½ cups of water, ginger and salt into the pot. Bring the mixture to a boil. Reduce the heat to low and cover the pot. Simmer for 20 minutes.
3. Add the coconut milk and continue to heat for 4 to 5 minutes.
4. Place the soup into a blender, blend it until creamy, working in batches if necessary and be careful about the hot liquid.
5. Serve.

Nutrition:

- Calories: 232
- Carbs: 15g
- Fat: 19g
- Protein: 3g

74. Garlic Pumpkin Soup with Fried Sage

- Serving Size: 4
- Preparation Time: 15 minutes
- Cooking Time: 10 minutes

Ingredients:

- 4 tbsp of extra-virgin olive oil
- 1 (15-ounce, 425 g) can of pumpkin purée
- 1 onion, chopped
- 2 garlic cloves, cut into ⅛-inch-thick slices
- 4 cups of vegetable broth
- 2 tsp of chipotle powder
- 1 tsp of salt
- ½ tsp of freshly ground black pepper
- ½ cup of vegetable oil
- 12 sage leaves, stemmed

Directions:

1. Add the olive oil, onion and garlic in a large, heavy Dutch over high heat and sauté for about 5 minutes, or until the vegetables begin to brown.
2. Then stir in the pumpkin, vegetable broth, chipotle powder, salt and pepper. Bring to a boil. Lower the heat to simmer and cook for 5 minutes.
3. Meanwhile, add the vegetable oil into a medium sauté pan and heat over high heat until hot.
4. Slide each sage leaf into the oil gently and cook for about 1 minute, or until it crisps. Transfer the sage to paper towels to drain with a slotted spoon. Once cool, discard the vegetable oil.
5. Place the soup into bowls (If you like you can purée the soup in a blender) and garnish each serving with 3 fried sage leaves.

Nutrition:

- Calories: 136
- Carbs: 45g
- Fat: 20g
- Protein: 10g

75. Classic Mediterranean Fish Stew

- Serving Size: 4
- Preparation Time: 15 minutes
- Cooking Time: 15 minutes

Ingredients:

- 2 pounds (907 g) firm white fish fillets, cut into 2-inch pieces
- 1 tbsp of extra-virgin olive oil, plus additional as needed
- 2 garlic cloves, minced
- 1 white onion, sliced thin
- 1 fennel bulb, sliced thin
- 1 tsp of ground cumin
- 1 tsp of ground oregano
- 1 (28-ounce, 794 g) can of crushed tomatoes
- Pinch saffron threads
- 1 tsp of salt
- ½ tsp of freshly ground black pepper
- 2 tbsp of chopped fresh parsley
- ½ lemon, for garnish

Directions:

1. Heat 1 tablespoon of olive oil in a large pot or pan over medium-high heat. Add the fennel, onion and garlic. Sauté for 5 minutes.
2. Stir in the cumin, saffron threads, oregano, crushed tomatoes, salt and pepper. Bring the mixture to a simmer.
3. Arrange the fish fillets in a single layer over the vegetables, cover the pan and simmer for 10 minutes.
4. Transfer the fish and vegetables to a serving platter.
5. Serve garnished with parsley, a drizzle of olive oil and a generous squeeze of lemon juice.

Nutrition:

- Calories: 362
- Carbs: 24g
- Fat: 21g
- Protein: 62g

76. Chilled Avocado Soup with Coconut Milk

- Serving Size: 6
- Preparation Time: 15 minutes plus 1 hour chilling,
- Cooking Time: 0

Ingredients:

- 3 ripe avocados, peeled and pitted
- ½ tsp of chopped fresh dill, plus fresh dill sprigs for garnish
- ¼ red onion, chopped, or about ¼ cup of precut packaged onion
- 1 garlic clove, crushed
- 1 tsp of grated fresh ginger
- 1 cup of Herbed Chicken Bone Broth
- 1 tbsp of freshly squeezed lemon juice
- 2 cups of canned low-fat coconut milk
- Sea salt
- Freshly ground black pepper
- Sliced radishes, for garnish

Directions:

1. Prepare the avocados, chop three of the four avocado halves coarsely and dice the remaining half, set it aside for garnish.
2. Add the chopped avocado, chopped dill, onion, garlic, ginger, chicken broth and lemon juice into a food processor. Purée them until very smooth. Place the avocado soup in a lidded container.
3. Pour in the coconut milk and whisk well.
4. Season with sea salt and pepper. Transfer the soup to the refrigerator to chill for at least 1 hour.
5. Garnish with the radishes, diced avocado and dill sprigs and serve.

Nutrition:

- Calories: 296
- Carbs: 14g
- Fat: 39g
- Protein: 4g

77. Cauliflower Soup with Onion

- Serving Size: 6
- Preparation Time: 10 minutes
- Cooking Time: 20 minutes

Ingredients:

- 1 tbsp of avocado oil
- 3 garlic cloves, minced
- 1 small white onion, diced
- 1 small celery root, trimmed, peeled and cut into 1-inch pieces
- 1 head cauliflower, roughly chopped into 1-inch pieces
- 2 tbsp of coconut oil
- 4 cups of vegetable broth
- 2 scallions, sliced

Directions:

1. In a soup pot, warm the avocado oil over medium heat.
2. Place the garlic and onion, sauté for 5 minutes.
3. Add the celery root and cauliflower. Increase the heat to medium-high and sauté for 5 minutes until the cauliflower gets brown and caramelized.
4. Stir in the coconut oil and broth and bring to a boil. Reduce the heat to medium-low and simmer for 10 minutes. Fetch the pot from the heat.
5. With an immersion blender, in batches in a blender, purée the soup until creamy.
6. Serve immediately, sprinkle with the scallions.

Nutrition:

- Calories: 187
- Carbs: 10g
- Fat: 8g
- Protein: 9g

78. Black Bean Stew with Mango and Onion

- Serving Size: 4
- Preparation Time: 10 minutes
- Cooking Time: 10 minutes

Ingredients:

- 2 tbsp of coconut oil
- 2 (15-ounce, 425 g) cans of black beans, drained and rinsed
- 1 onion, chopped
- 2 ripe mangoes, sliced thin
- ¼ cup of chopped fresh cilantro, divided
- ¼ cup of sliced scallions, divided
- 1 tbsp of chili powder
- 1 tsp of salt
- ¼ tsp of freshly ground black pepper
- 1 cup of water

Directions:

1. Add the coconut oil into a large pot and melt over high heat.
2. Place the onion into the pot and sauté for 5 minutes.
3. Stir in the black beans, chili powder, salt, pepper and water. Bring to a boil. Lower the heat to simmer and cook for 5 minutes.
4. Take the pot off the heat; stir in the mangoes just before serving. Garnish each serving with cilantro and scallions.

Nutrition:

- Calories: 243
- Carbs: 72g
- Fat: 9g
- Protein: 20g

79. Creamy Sweet Potato Onion Curry Soup

- Serving Size: 4
- Preparation Time: 10 minutes
- Cooking Time: 15 minutes

Ingredients:

- 2 tbsp of extra-virgin olive oil
- 1 onion, chopped
- 1 tsp of ground turmeric
- 4 cups of cubed, peeled sweet potato
- 8 cups of no-salt-added vegetable broth
- 1 tsp of curry powder
- ⅛ tsp of freshly ground black pepper
- ½ tsp of sea salt

Directions:

1. Heat the olive oil in a large pot over medium-high heat, until it shimmers.
2. Stir in the onion. Cook until soft, about 5 minutes, stirring occasionally.
3. Add the turmeric, sweet potato, vegetable broth, curry powder, pepper and salt, stir well and bring the mixture to a boil. Lower the heat to medium and simmer for about 10 minutes until the sweet potato cubes are soft.
4. Transfer the mixture to a blender and blend until smooth.
5. Serve.

Nutrition:

- Calories: 256
- Carbs: 45g
- Fat: 7g
- Protein: 3g

80. Garlicky Carrot Ginger Soup with Lentil

- Serving Size: 4-6
- Preparation Time: 15 minutes
- Cooking Time: 10 minutes

Ingredients:

- 1 tbsp of coconut oil
- 1 (15-ounce, 425 g) can of lentils, drained and rinsed
- 2 carrots, sliced thin
- 1 small white onion, peeled and sliced thin
- 2 garlic cloves, peeled and sliced thin
- 1 tbsp of chopped fresh ginger
- 3 cups of water, or vegetable broth
- 2 tbsp of chopped fresh cilantro, or parsley
- 1 tsp of salt
- ¼ tsp of freshly ground black pepper

Directions:

1. Add the coconut oil into a large pot and melt over medium-high heat. Add the carrots, onion, garlic and ginger. Sauté for 5 minutes.
2. Pour the water into the pot and bring to a boil. Lower the heat to simmer and cook until the carrots are tender, about 5 minutes.
3. Stir in the lentils, cilantro, salt and pepper.
4. Serve.

Nutrition:

- Calories: 173
- Carbs: 28g
- Fat: 5g
- Protein: 14g

81. Cream Broccoli Kale Soup

- Serving Size: 4
- Preparation Time: 10 minutes
- Cooking Time: 20 minutes

Ingredients:

- 2 tbsp of extra-virgin olive oil, plus extra for garnish, if desired
- 1 onion, finely chopped
- 1 cup of broccoli florets
- 4 cups of kale
- 6 cups of no-salt vegetable broth
- 1 tsp of garlic powder
- ¼ tsp of freshly ground black pepper
- ½ tsp of sea salt
- microgreens (optional)
- unsweetened coconut milk (optional)

Directions:

1. Heat the olive oil in a large pot over medium-high heat, until it shimmers.
2. Stir in the onion and cook for about 5 minutes, until it is soft.
3. Stir in broccoli, kale, vegetable broth, garlic powder, pepper and salt. Bring to a boil and reduce the heat to medium-low. Simmer until the vegetables are soft, about 10 to 15 minutes.
4. Transfer the soup to a blender and blend until smooth. Serve hot with the microgreens (if using), additional oil and coconut milk (if using).

Nutrition:

- Calories: 275
- Carbs: 16g
- Fat: 7g
- Protein: 3g

82. Garlic French Onion Soup

- Serving Size: 4
- Preparation Time: 15 minutes
- Cooking Time: 2 hours, 30 minutes

Ingredients:

- 2 tbsp of olive oil
- 2 tsp of bottled minced garlic
- 3 pounds (1.4 kg) of sweet onions, halved and cut into ⅛-inch-thick slices
- ½ cup of dry sherry
- 1 tbsp of chopped fresh thyme
- 8 cups of Beef Bone Broth
- Freshly ground black pepper
- Sea salt

Directions:

1. Heat the olive oil in a large stockpot over low heat.
2. Place the garlic and onions in the pot. Cover and cook for 30 minutes, allowing the juices to purge from the onions. Stir occasionally.
3. Remove the lid. Continue to sauté the garlic and onions for about 1 hour, 30 minutes, or until they are a deep caramel color, stirring occasionally.
4. Mix in the sherry to deglaze the pan, scraping up any browned bits from the bottom.
5. Increase the heat to medium. Add the thyme and beef broth. Bring to a boil. Reduce the heat to low and simmer until the onions are tender about 30 minutes.
6. Use pepper and sea salt to season. And serve.

Nutrition:

- Calories: 253
- Carbs: 33g
- Fat: 9g
- Protein: 9g

83. Creamy Sweet Potato Soup

- Serving Size: 6
- Preparation Time: 15 minutes
- Cooking Time: 35 minutes

Ingredients:

- 1 tbsp of olive oil
- 2 tsp of grated fresh ginger
- 1 sweet onion, chopped, or about 1 cup of precut packaged onion
- 2 pounds (907 g) sweet potatoes (about 4), peeled and diced, or 6 cups of precut packaged sweet potatoes
- 1 carrot, diced, or ¾ cup of precut packaged carrots
- 8 cups of Herbed Chicken Bone Broth
- 1 tsp of ground cinnamon
- ¼ cup of pure maple syrup
- ¼ tsp of ground nutmeg
- 1 cup of coconut cream, plus 1 tbsp for garnish
- Sea salt to taste

Directions:

1. Heat the olive oil in a large stockpot over medium-high heat.
2. Stir in the ginger and onion. Sauté until softened, about 3 minutes.
3. Add the sweet potatoes, carrot, chicken broth, cinnamon, maple syrup and nutmeg. Bring to a boil. Reduce the heat to low and simmer until the vegetables are tender about 30 minutes.
4. In a food processor, purée the soup, in batches, until very smooth. Return the soup to the pot.
5. Add the coconut cream, stir well and reheat the soup.
6. With sea salt to season, drizzle coconut cream over and garnish with a fresh herb of your choice and serve.

Nutrition:

- Calories: 404
- Carbs: 58g
- Fat: 13g
- Protein: 5g

84. Ginger Butternut Squash Soup

- Serving Size: 4
- Preparation Time: 10 minutes
- Cooking Time: 20 minutes

Ingredients:

- 2 tbsp of extra-virgin olive oil
- 1 tbsp of grated ginger
- 1 onion, chopped
- 4 garlic cloves, minced
- 3 cups of butternut squash
- 6 cups of vegetable broth
- ¼ tsp of freshly ground black pepper
- ½ tsp of sea salt
- ¼ cup of unsweetened coconut milk (optional)
- ¼ cup of microgreens (optional)

Directions:

1. Heat the olive oil in a large pot over medium-high heat, until it shimmers.
2. Stir in the ginger and onion and cook until the onion is soft, about 5 minutes, stirring occasionally.
3. Place the garlic in the pot and cook for another 30 seconds, stirring constantly.
4. Stir in the squash, vegetable broth, pepper and salt. Covered and cook until the squash is soft (about 10 minutes).
5. Remove them from the pot and transfer them to a blender. Blend until smooth.
6. Garnished with coconut milk and microgreens, if using, serve.

Nutrition:

- Calories: 175
- Carbs: 9g
- Fat: 7g
- Protein: 1g

85. Easy Mixed Vegetable Noodle Bowl

- Serving Size: 4
- Preparation Time: 20 minutes
- Cooking Time: 20 minutes

Ingredients:

- 1 large carrot, julienned or spiralized
- 1 parsnip, julienned or spiralized
- 1 cup of shredded bok choy
- 1 cup of bean sprouts
- ¼ sweet onion, or about ¼ cup of precut packaged onion
- 1 tbsp of raw honey
- 3 cups of canned unsweetened coconut milk
- 1 cup of low-sodium vegetable broth
- 1 tbsp of coconut aminos
- 3 garlic cloves
- 1 (2-inch) piece fresh ginger, peeled
- Juice of 1 lime (1 or 2 tbsp of)
- 2 tbsp of chopped fresh cilantro
- Zest of 1 lime (optional)

Directions:

1. Add the coconut aminos, honey, coconut milk, vegetable broth, garlic, onion, lime juice, lime zest (if using) and ginger into a blender and pulse until puréed. Transfer the mixture to a large saucepan and bring to a boil over high heat. Reduce the heat to low and simmer for 15 minutes.
2. Add the bok choy, carrot, bean sprouts and parsnip, stir well and simmer until the vegetables are tender, about 4 minutes.
3. Top with the cilantro and serve.

Nutrition:

- Calories: 280
- Carbs: 25g
- Fat: 10g
- Protein: 6g

86. Fish and Shrimp Soup

- Serving Size: 6
- Preparation Time: 15 minutes
- Cooking Time: 25 minutes

Ingredients:

- 1 tbsp of olive oil
- 1 pound (454 g) haddock, cut into 1-inch pieces
- ½ pound (227 g) peeled and deveined shrimp, chopped
- 1 sweet onion, chopped, or about 1 cup of precut packaged onion
- 2 stalks of celery, chopped, or about ¾ to 1 cup of precut packaged celery
- 2 cups of cubed sweet potato
- 2 carrots, diced, or about 1½ cups of precut packaged carrots
- 2 tsp of bottled minced garlic
- 6 cups of Herbed Chicken Bone Broth
- ½ tsp of ground cumin
- ½ tsp of ground coriander
- 1 cup of fresh spinach
- 2 tbsp of chopped fresh cilantro

Directions:

1. Heat the olive oil in a large stockpot over medium-high heat.
2. Stir in the garlic, onion and celery. Sauté until softened, about 3 minutes.
3. Add the carrots, sweet potato, cumin, coriander and chicken broth. Bring the soup to a boil. Reduce the heat to low and simmer until the vegetables are tender about 10 minutes.
4. Add the shrimp and haddock. Simmer for another 10 minutes.
5. Add the spinach and simmer for 2 minutes.
6. Top the soup with the cilantro and serve.

Nutrition:

- Calories: 232
- Carbs: 20g
- Fat: 8g
- Protein: 26g

87. Garlicky Ginger Potato and Rice Soup

- Serving Size: 4-6
- Preparation Time: 15 minutes
- Cooking Time: 15 minutes

Ingredients:

- 1 large sweet potato, peeled and cut into 1-inch cubes
- 4 cups of vegetable broth
- 1 bunch broccolini, cut into 1-inch pieces
- 2 onions, coarsely chopped
- 2 garlic cloves, sliced thin
- 2 tsp of minced fresh ginger
- 1 cup of cooked Arborio rice
- ¼ cup of fresh cilantro leaves

Directions:

1. Add the broth into a large Dutch oven and bring to a boil over high heat.
2. Place the sweet potato, onion, garlic and ginger into the oven and simmer for 5 to 8 minutes, or until the sweet potato is cooked through.
3. Stir in the broccolini and simmer for another 3 minutes.
4. Take the pan off the heat. Mix in the rice and cilantro and serve.

Nutrition:

- Calories: 172
- Carbs: 29g
- Fat: 2g
- Protein: 8g

88. Apple Crisp

- Serving Size: 12
- Preparation Time: 30 minutes
- Cooking Time: 45 minutes

Ingredients:

- Crust/Crumble
- 1 cup of rolled oats
- 1 cup of whole wheat flour
- ½ cup of Grape Nuts cereal
- 1 teaspoon of cinnamon
- 1 cup of unsweetened apple juice
- Filling
- 2 apples, sliced
- ½ cup of raisins
- 1 cup of unsweetened apple juice
- 2 teaspoons of cinnamon
- 1 tablespoon of lemon juice
- 2 teaspoons of cornstarch

Directions:

1. Preheat oven to 350°F.
2. Combine all crust/crumble ingredients and press half of the mixture into the bottom of a 9-inch nonstick pan and bake for 5 minutes. Remove from oven and set aside.
3. Raise oven to 375°F.
4. In a saucepan combine apples, raisins, apple juice, cinnamon, lemon juice and cornstarch and boil for 10 minutes.
5. Remove apples and raisins, place them in the prepared crust and reduce liquid until thick, approximately 5 minutes.
6. Pour liquid into the crust and top with the remaining crumble mixture.
7. Bake for 30 minutes.
8. Divide into portions and serve.

Nutrition:

- Calories: 100
- Carbs: 20g
- Fat: 1g
- Protein: 3g

89. Avocado Tuna Bites

- Serving Size: 4
- Preparation Time: 10 minutes
- Cooking Time: 5 minutes

Ingredients:

- 1/3 cup of coconut oil
- 1 avocado, cut into cubes
- 10 ounces canned tuna, drained
- ¼ cup of parmesan cheese, grated
- ¼ teaspoon of garlic powder
- 1/4 teaspoon of onion powder
- 1/3 cup of almond flour
- ¼ teaspoon of pepper
- ¼ cup of low-fat mayonnaise
- Pepper as needed

Directions:

1. Take a bowl and add tuna, mayo, flour, parmesan and spices and mix well.
2. Fold in avocado and make 12 balls out of the mixture.
3. Melt coconut oil in a pan and cook over medium heat, until all sides are golden.
4. Serve and enjoy!

Nutrition:

- Calories: 185
- Carbs: 1g
- Fat: 18g
- Protein: 5g

90. Baked Eggplant Chips with Salad and Aioli

- Serving Size: 4
- Preparation Time: 15 minutes
- Cooking Time: 30 minutes

Ingredients:

- 2 eggplants, sliced
- 1 egg, beaten
- 3 1/2 oz of cooked beets shred
- 3 1/2 oz of red cabbage shred
- 2 cups of almond meal
- 2 tbsp of butter, melted
- 2 egg yolks
- 2 cloves of garlic, chopped
- 1 cup of olive oil
- 1/2 1 tsp of red chili flakes
- 2 tbsp of lemon juice
- 3 tbsp of yogurt
- 2 tablespoons of fresh cilantro chopped
- Black pepper and salt to taste

Directions:

1. Preheat the oven to 400 F. On a thick plate, make a mixture of flour, salt and pepper. Dip the eggplants in the egg and then dip them in the flour. Place them on a baking sheet and then brush them with butter. Cook for about 15 minutes
2. For aioli to make, whisk egg yolks and garlic. Gradually add 3 cups of olive oil as you whisk. Add chili flakes, salt pepper, 1 tbsp of lemon juice and yogurt. In a bowl for salad, mix cabbage, beets, cilantro, the rest of the oil, the remaining lemon juice, salt and pepper. Toss in a dressing.
3. Serve the fries alongside Aioli and the beet salad.

Nutrition:

- Calories: 377
- Carbs: 10.5g
- Fat: 65g
- Protein: 8g

91. Baked Scotch Eggs

- Serving Size: 4
- Preparation Time: 20 minutes
- Cooking Time: 35 minutes

Ingredients:

- 4 eggs, hard-boiled
- 1 egg
- 1/2 cup of pork rinds, crushed
- 1 lb pork sausages, skinless
- 2 tbsp of Grana Padano, grated
- 1 clove of garlic, chopped
- 1/2 teaspoon of onion powder
- 1/2 tsp of cayenne pepper
- 1 tsp of fresh chopped parsley chopped
- Black pepper and salt to taste

Directions:

1. Preheat the oven to 350 F. Within a mixing dish, mix all the ingredients, except for the egg and the pork rinds. Grab a few tablespoons from the sausage mixture and put it in each of the eggs.
2. Utilizing your fingers, you can mold the mixture until it's sealed. Mix the egg using a fork in the bowl. Dip the sausage eggs into the egg, coat them with pork rinds and put them in a baking dish. Bake for 25 minutes or until crisp and golden brown.
3. Serve.

Nutrition:

- Calories: 265
- Carbs: 1.1g
- Fat: 15g
- Protein: 29g

92. Cashew and Carrot Muffins

- Serving Size: 4
- Preparation Time: 10 minutes
- Cooking Time: 3 hours

Ingredients:

- 4 tablespoons cashew butter, melted
- 4 eggs, whisked
- ½ cup of coconut cream
- 1 cup of carrots, peeled and grated
- 4 teaspoons maple syrup
- ¾ cup of coconut flour
- ½ teaspoon of baking soda

Directions:

1. In a bowl, mix the cashew butter with the eggs, cream and the other ingredients, whisk well and pour into a muffin pan that fits the slow cooker.
2. Put the lid on, cook the muffins on High for 3 hours, cool down and serve.

Nutrition:

- Calories: 245
- Carbs: 28.6g
- Fat: 21.7g
- Protein: 12.3g

93. Cheese and Nut Zucchini Boats

- Serving Size: 4
- Preparation Time: 20 minutes
- Cooking Time: 35 minutes

Ingredients:

- 2 medium zucchinis, halved
- 1 cup of cauliflower rice
- 2 tbsp of olive oil
- 1/4 cup of vegetable broth
- 1 1/4 cups of diced tomatoes
- 1 red onion chopped
- 1 cup of pine nuts
- 1/4 cup of hazelnuts
- 1 tablespoon of balsamic vinegar
- 1 tbsp of smoked paprika
- 1 cup of grated Monterey Jack
- 4 tbsp of chopped cilantro

Directions:

1. Preheat the oven to 350 F. Put the cauli rice, broth and cauli in an oven-proof pot. Cook for up to 5 minutes Then, you can fluff the rice and let it cool. Scoop the pulp out of the zucchini halves, then slice the flesh.
2. The zucchini shells should be brushed with olive oil. In a bowl, mix cauli rice, tomatoes, red onion, hazelnuts, pine nuts, cilantro, vinegar and paprika and the zucchini pulp. Pour the mix into the zucchini halves. Drizzle with the remaining prepared olive oil, then sprinkle the cheese over. Then bake for approximately around 20 minutes, or until the cheese is melted.
3. Serve.

Nutrition:

- Calories: 228
- Carbs: 7g
- Fat: 31g
- Protein: 12g

94. Cheese Chips

- Serving Size: 8
- Preparation Time: 15 minutes
- Cooking Time: 15 minutes

Ingredients:

- 3 tablespoons of coconut flour
- ½ cup of strong cheddar cheese, grated and divided
- ¼ cup of Parmesan cheese, grated
- 2 tablespoons of butter melted
- 1 egg
- 1 teaspoon of fresh thyme leaves, minced

Directions:

1. Preheat the oven to 350o F. Line a large baking sheet with parchment paper.
2. In a bowl, place the coconut flour, ¼ cup of grated cheddar, Parmesan, butter and egg and mix until well combined.
3. Set the mixture aside for about 3-5 minutes.
4. Make 8 equal-sized balls from the mixture.
5. Arrange the prepared balls onto the prepared baking sheet in a single layer about 2 inches apart.
6. With your hands, press each ball into a little flat disc.
7. Sprinkle each disc with the remaining cheddar, followed by thyme.
8. Bake for about 13-15 minutes or until the edges become golden brown.
9. Remove from the preheated oven and let them cool completely before serving.

Nutrition:

- Calories: 189
- Carbs: 4g
- Fat: 28g
- Protein: 14g

95. Cheesy Mashed Sweet Potato Cakes

- Serving Size: 4
- Preparation Time: 10 minutes
- Cooking Time: 30 minutes

Ingredients:

- ¾ cup of breadcrumbs
- 4 cups of mashed potatoes
- ½ cup of onions
- 2 cups of grated mozzarella cheese
- ¼ cup of freshly grated parmesan cheese
- 2 large cloves finely chopped
- 1 egg
- 2 teaspoons finely chopped parsley
- Salt and pepper to taste

Directions:

1. Line your baking sheet with foil. Wash, peel and cut the prepared sweet potatoes into 6 pieces. Arrange them inside the baking sheet and drizzle a small amount of oil on top before seasoning with salt and pepper.
2. Cover with a baking sheet and bake it for 45 minutes. Once cooked transfer them into a mixing bowl and mash them well with a potato masher.
3. To the sweet potatoes in a bowl add green onions, parmesan, mozzarella, garlic, egg, parsley and breadcrumbs. Mash and combine the mixture together using the masher.
4. Put the remaining ¼ cup of the breadcrumbs in a place. Scoop a teaspoon of mixture into your palm and form round patties around ½ an inch thick. Dredge your patties in the breadcrumbs to cover both sides and set them aside.
5. Heat a tablespoon of oil in a medium nonstick pan. When the oil is hot, begin to cook the patties in batches 4 or 5 per session and cook each side for 6 minutes until they turn golden brown. Using a spoon or spatula flip them. Add oil to prevent burning.
6. Divide into portions and serve.

Nutrition:

- Calories: 126
- Carbs: 15g
- Fat: 6g
- Proteins: 3g

96. Cherry Clafouti

- Serving Size: 6
- Preparation Time: 30 minutes
- Cooking Time: 45 minutes

Ingredients:

- ¼ cup of + 2 teaspoons flour
- ½ teaspoon of baking powder
- ¼ cup of egg substitute
- 2 egg whites
- 1/3 cup of Splenda
- ½ cup of cherry or pomegranate juice
- 2½ cups of frozen cherries, thawed and chopped
- Zest of 1 orange

Directions:

1. Preheat oven to 375°F.
2. Spray an 8-inch baking dish with cooking spray.
3. In a medium-sized bowl, combine flour and baking powder.
4. In a separate medium-sized bowl, combine egg substitute and egg whites; whip until frothy; add in Splenda, juice and flour mixture; and mix until smooth and blended.
5. Fold in cherries and zest and ladle into baking dish; bake for 35–45 minutes until golden brown.
6. Allow to cool and serve with fat-free vanilla, frozen yogurt, or a dollop of low-fat whipped topping.

Nutrition:

- Calories: 140, Carbs: 30g, Fat: 0.5g, Protein: 4g

97. Cinnamon Peach Cobbler

- Serving Size: 4
- Preparation Time: 10 minutes
- Cooking Time: 4 hours

Ingredients:

- 4 cups of peaches, peeled and sliced
- Cooking spray
- ¼ cup of coconut sugar
- 1 and ½ cups of whole wheat sweet crackers, crushed
- ½ cup of almond milk
- ½ teaspoon of cinnamon powder
- ¼ cup of stevia
- 1 teaspoon of vanilla extract
- ¼ teaspoon of nutmeg, ground

Directions:

1. In a bowl, mix peaches with sugar, cinnamon and stir.
2. In a separate bowl, mix crackers with stevia, nutmeg, almond milk and vanilla extract and stir.
3. Spray your slow cooker with cooking spray, spread peaches on the bottom and add the crackers mix, spread, cover and cook on Low for 4 hours.
4. Divide into bowls and serve.

Nutrition:

- Calories: 249
- Carbs: 42.7g
- Fat: 11.4g
- Protein: 3.5g

98. Fat-Free Fries

- Serving Size: 2
- Preparation Time: 20 minutes
- Cooking Time: 20 minutes

Ingredients:

- Butter-flavored nonfat cooking spray
- 2 large Yukon gold potatoes, cut thin into fries
- 2 egg whites, beaten
- Salt and pepper to taste
- Toasted garlic powder
- Ground red chili flakes
- Fresh minced chives

Directions:

1. Thoroughly spray a nonstick baking sheet with butter-flavored cooking spray.
2. Coat potatoes in egg whites and lay out a single layer on a sheet pan.
3. Sprinkle with salt and pepper, garlic powder and chili flakes.
4. Bake at 350°F for 20 minutes, adding chives when almost done.
5. Divide into portions and serve.

Nutrition:

- Calories: 260
- Carbs: 53g
- Fat: 0g
- Protein: 11g

99. Ginger and Pumpkin Pie

- Serving Size: 10
- Preparation Time: 10 minutes
- Cooking Time: 2 hours

Ingredients:

- 2 cups of almond flour
- 1 egg, whisked
- 1 cup of pumpkin puree
- 1 and ½ teaspoons baking powder
- Cooking spray
- 1 tablespoon of coconut oil, melted
- 1 tablespoon of vanilla extract
- ½ teaspoon of baking soda
- 1 and ½ teaspoons of cinnamon powder
- ¼ teaspoon of ginger, ground
- 1/3 cup of maple syrup
- 1 teaspoon of lemon juice

Directions:

1. In a bowl, flour with baking powder, baking soda, cinnamon, ginger, egg, oil, vanilla, pumpkin puree, maple syrup and lemon juice, stir and pour in your slow cooker greased with cooking spray and lined with parchment paper, cover the pot and cook on low for 2 hours and 20 minutes.
2. Leave the pie to cool down, slice and serve.

Nutrition:

- Calories: 191
- Carbs: 10.8g
- Fat: 4.8g
- Protein: 2g

100. Ginger Snaps

- Serving Size: 18
- Preparation Time: 15 minutes
- Cooking Time: 10 minutes

Ingredients:

- 4 tablespoons of unsalted butter
- 1/2 cup of light brown sugar
- 2 tablespoons of molasses
- 1 egg white
- 2 1/2 teaspoons of ground ginger
- 1/4 teaspoon of ground allspice
- 1 teaspoon of sodium-free baking soda
- 1/2 cup of unbleached all-purpose flour
- 12 cups of white whole-wheat flour
- 1 tablespoon of sugar

Directions:

1. Warm oven to 375°F. Put aside a baking sheet with parchment paper. Put the butter, sugar and molasses into a mixing bowl and beat well.
2. Mix the egg white, ginger and allspice. Mix in the baking soda, then put in the flour, then beat.
3. Roll the dough into small balls. Put the balls on a prepared baking sheet and press down using a glass dipped in a tablespoon of sugar.
4. Once the glass presses on the dough, it will moisten sufficiently to coat with sugar. Bake within 10 minutes. Let it cool, then serve.

Nutrition:

- Calories: 81
- Carbs: 14g
- Fat: 2g
- Protein: 1g

101. Goat Cheese and Rutabaga Puffs

- Serving Size: 4
- Preparation Time: 20 minutes
- Cooking Time: 35 minutes

Ingredients:

- 1/2 oz goat cheese, crumbled
- 1 rutabaga, peeled and cut into pieces
- 2 tablespoons of butter that is melted
- One cup of ground pork rinds

Directions:

1. Preheat the oven to 350 F. Spread rutabaga on baking sheets and drizzle with butter. Roast until soft, about 15 minutes. Transfer the cooked vegetables to an ice cube. Let it cool before adding goat cheese.
2. Utilizing a fork, mash to mix all the components. Put the pork rinds on the plate. Form 1-inch balls from the rutabaga and then wrap them around the rinds, pressing them lightly to adhere. Put them on the baking pan and cook for about 10 minutes or until golden.
3. Divide into portions and serve.

Nutrition:

- Calories: 131
- Carbs: 5.9g
- Fat: 9g
- Protein: 3g

CONCLUSION

There are a lot of diets out there that claim to help you lose weight quickly and easily. Some of them even claim they will help you lose weight without dieting.

It's not true. If you want to be healthy and maintain a healthy weight, then you will have to put in at least some effort on your own behalf. It's easy enough that anyone can do it.

It may work in the short term when you see quick results, but it will not last long. After a few weeks without any form of physical activity and eating these small amounts, you are bound to gain weight again.

This is where calories come into play. It is important that you not only pay attention to what you are eating but also how much you are eating.

Calories are the energy that your body needs to function properly, which is why it is so important to keep track of what goes into your body.

This can be accomplished by having a diet program that reminds you of the nutritional values of certain foods, such as calories and carbs.

You can then add them up at the end of each meal and subtract them from the total amount of calories you have available for that day. That way, you will know how much you can eat for the day without going over your calories.

If you do go over your calories for that day, then you may have to work out more in order to burn off the excess calories.

You can also use a calorie counter on the Internet or an app on your phone which can help track the number of calories that are in each food that you are eating.

Here we depart. I hope this cookbook serves you well in your journey to a healthier life.

Printed in Great Britain
by Amazon

43290946R00059